INTERNATIONAL PERSPECTIVES OF MILITARY LEADERSHIP

IN PURSUIT OF EXCELLENCE:

INTERNATIONAL PERSPECTIVES OF MILITARY LEADERSHIP

Edited by:

Colonel Bernd Horn and
Lieutenant-Colonel Allister MacIntyre

CANADIAN DEFENCE ACADEMY PRESS

Canadian Defence Academy Press
PO Box 17000 Stn Forces
Kingston, Ontario K7K 7B4

Produced for the Canadian Defence Academy Press
by 17 Wing Winnipeg Publishing Office.
WPO30208

Cover Photo: Silvia Pecota

Library and Archives Canada Cataloguing in Publication

In pursuit of excellence : international perspectives of military leadership/edited by Colonel Bernd Horn and Lieutenant-Colonel Allister MacIntyre.

Issued by Canadian Defence Academy.
Includes bibliographical references.
ISBN 0-662-43939-2
Cat. no.: D2-182/2006E

1. Command of troops. 2. Leadership. I. Horn, Bernd, 1959-
II. MacIntyre, Allister T. (Allister Tompkins), 1954- III. Canadian Defence Academy IV. Title: International perspectives of military leadership.

UB210.I53 2006 355.3'3041 C2006-980207-6

UA600.O63 2006 355.30971 C2006-980116-9

Printed in Canada.

3 5 7 9 10 8 6 4 2

TABLE OF CONTENTS

FOREWORD

I am delighted to introduce *In Pursuit of Excellence: International Perspectives of Military Leadership*, which represents the latest of our CDA Press publications. This book is of special significance as it represents the outcome of international collaboration. Although CDA Press was established to provide a venue for Canadian researchers and scholars, as well as a vehicle for the creation and promulgation of a distinct Canadian body of operational knowledge centred on leadership and the profession of arms, one cannot ignore the benefits of external research and perspectives. As such, this book provides a wealth of information and insight.

In Pursuit of Excellence represents one of the first products stemming from an inaugural meeting of a number of leadership centres from Australia, Canada, England, Korea, New Zealand, Singapore and the United States of America that gathered in November 2005 in Singapore to discuss possible venues for collaborative research. As a result of these initial efforts, a number of concrete steps were taken. Significantly, Singapore's SAFTI Training Institute undertook to establish a community of practice website for leadership centres that would provide a continual conduit of cooperation and dialogue. In addition, through the Canadian Forces Leadership Institute, CDA took responsibility for producing this volume.

Both initiatives are seminal in advancing international cooperation in the field of military leadership. This is of great importance. Often we become constrained in our thinking by our own cultural, regional and philosophical baggage. As such, dialogue and cooperation with allies, partners and other international colleagues opens up horizons and insights that may have been lost. The experience only enriches us all.

As an example of that cooperation, this book provides a window into the leadership doctrine and experience of four different militaries. As a result, readers will be able to discover the components, catalysts and foundational theories of military leadership in a number of different countries around the world. This insight may assist in the development or refinement of parallel research in other nations, or it may just add to a better understanding of other cultures and armed forces. As our network of military leadership partners expands, and becomes more formalized, we anticipate that the potential benefits will multiply. We also suspect that this volume will be joined by subsequent international publications that will highlight our collaborative efforts and help to draw attention to the importance of military leadership.

In closing, I believe you will find this book of great interest and of immense value. Please do not hesitate to contact us at the Canadian Defence Academy if you wish to discuss issues that arise in the book, or simply if you wish to explore collaborative ventures with us.

Major-General P.R. Hussey
Commander
Canadian Defence Academy

INTRODUCTION

The importance of leadership, whether in business, politics, sports, the public service or the military, is universally understood. Ironically, even though most would agree that leadership is one of the most critical ingredients for an organization's success, there remains, to this day, no clear agreement on its definition or application. In fact, scholars have been debating concepts of leadership for centuries. For example, the "Great Man" approach emerged in the 19th century in response to Thomas Carlyle's comment that the world's history is nothing more than the biographies of great men. This approach, with its emphasis on the traits, attributes, and characteristics of leaders, has fallen out of favour. Most modern historians understand that the decisions of any individual have less importance to history than economic, societal, technological, political, and environmental influences. Controversy continues to swirl around the debate on whether leaders are born or created. Adding to the perplexity is the confusion many have in regards to the differences between management, leadership and command.

Especially incredulous is the fact that literally hundreds of books on leadership have been published without the inclusion of a concrete definition of what the authors were referring to as leadership. Frequently, it is just assumed that when discussing leadership everyone inherently knows what is meant. The reasoning is often, "I don't know how to explain it, but I certainly recognize it when I see it." Nowhere is this truer than in the military where a degree of arrogance is at play. Military commanders at all levels are insulted by the inference that they may have something to learn about leadership – after all, they live it every day!

But alas, the consequence of this apathy is that leadership is not always well understood, in theory or in practice. If we take the time to explore people's perceptions of leadership, and closely examine the multitude of definitions that have been enunciated, we are able to find some common ground and, conversely, some not so common ground. We discover that everyone agrees that leadership cannot take place in the absence of followers. Most are willing to admit that leadership is an influence process where a leader imposes his or her will to achieve some objective. Many categorize this influence as being either task or people oriented, with little agreement on whether it can simultaneously be both. Countless perspectives focus on leadership styles, with only a modicum of consensus on what these styles should look like. Some approaches are situationally based with the argument that leaders must adjust their styles to the situation, while others take a contingency approach and insist that success is *contingent* upon having the right leader in the right place at the right time.

Regardless of the viewpoint taken, it is apparent that there is a widespread interest in leadership at the organizational level. Leadership training programs are proliferated throughout industry, and the leadership related themes are abundantly apparent in the vision statements and mottos offered by countless companies. Nevertheless, surprisingly few individual leaders take the time to fully understand the principles of leadership, nor do they take the necessary steps to ensure that their leadership skills are developed, honed, and maintained to maximize their effectiveness. As implied earlier, the outcome of this lack of interest is fairly universal – failure. Unfortunately, it is normally only as a reaction to failure that the necessary corrective actions are taken. Significantly, the more catastrophic the failure, the more momentous is the corresponding corrective action.

In the end, the importance of leadership to organizational success is undeniable. Therefore, it is not surprising that organizations in the entire societal spectrum have invested so much time and effort into understanding its complexities to better master its application. The military has been no different. Arguably, there is no domain where leadership is more critical. What vocation or profession could possibly carry more consequence than leading a nation's sons and daughters in the defence of the country? For this reason, many militaries around the world have invested resources in studying leadership so that it can be more completely understood and more effectively applied. Some militaries have taken these steps as a consequence of failure, while others are investing their resources in leadership to avoid experiencing a similar fate. Either way, motives aside, the most significant aspect of this trend is the recognition within the militaries of the world that leadership is critical.

In this vein, *In Pursuit of Excellence: International Perspectives of Military Leadership* opens an international window on the rationale and foundational premises of leadership theory in four separate militaries – Australian, British, Canadian and Singaporean. As a result, readers can glean how these countries have faced their leadership challenges. Additionally, readers will gain an appreciation into the differences and similarities in the views of leadership as espoused in the approaches taken by the countries. Finally, insights into leadership theory and application, as well as an understanding of the dynamics of how the countries reached their doctrinal foundation will emerge.

This book in itself is representative of the dynamic international focus on the study of leadership. It is the cooperative venture of the first inaugural meeting of a number of leadership centres from Australia, Canada, England, Korea, New Zealand, Singapore and the United States of America that took place in November 2005 in Singapore. The military leadership centres came together to discuss possible venues for collaborative research and discovered that they were facing similar hurdles and striving for comparable goals. They have since formed a more permanent association that continues to grow and attract other members. This is seminal. Predictably, we all become constrained in our thinking based on our individual and societal biases and experiences. This often restricts our ability to break through invisible walls that impede exploration down different hallways and alleys. However, international dialogue and collaboration breaks down these indiscernible barriers and opens up greater understanding and a more holistic perspective. Moreover, it allows the possibility to enhance and/or improve organizational leadership doctrine, regardless of whether we come from a military, business, sports, private or public sector.

In the end, this seminal pilot initiative is offered as a means to expand the body of knowledge on leadership. It provides an in-depth perspective of the doctrinal leadership base of four militaries around the world. In reading this volume, the contributors hope that you will gain a better understanding of leadership in general, and of the respective national approach, in detail. We hope that *In Pursuit of Excellence* generates interest and debate on the subject of leadership, as well as increases interest by other leadership centres around the world.

CHAPTER 1

In Pursuit of the Capability Edge: Perspectives On the Australian Defence Force Leadership Development Experience

Jamie Cullens and Peter Kelly[1]

The Australian Army was like the post - Versailles German Army…men in the ranks could have been leaders.

General William Westmoreland, US Army, Vietnam

In 1996, Professor Fred Fiedler, one of the world's most prolific researchers and writers, reviewed half a century of leadership research for a prestigious academic business journal. "If leadership were easy to understand," he remarked, "we would have had all the answers long before now….We do know a good deal more about leadership today than we did 40 years ago, but without doubt, we still have a lot to learn." These remarks neatly encapsulate the Australian Defence Force's (ADF) situation with respect to leadership training and development. ADF leadership has many strengths and these continue to be tested on operations that since 1999 have included East Timor, Bougainville, Iraq, Bali, the Sudan, the Solomons, Sumatra and Afghanistan. However, anecdotal reports and official investigations, as well as some extensive survey evidence, suggest that there are also a number of weaknesses. This should not be surprising since demands on leaders at all levels in the ADF are greater than they have ever been.

In 1999, Brigadier Kevin O'Brien conducted a study on the provision of leadership development in the ADF and drew

[1] DISCLAIMER - the views expressed in this chapter are those of the authors and not the Australian Department of Defence.

some interesting conclusions that remain true to this day. He observed that organisations that rely on technology or physical infrastructure for their competitive edge are generally deluding themselves. He argues that anyone can buy the hardware and software. The key, he argued, lies in people who deal with the customers and the people who develop innovations, or, exploit their potential. In the military context, there is a proliferation of leading edge technologies available to those nations who can afford them, and, increasingly these weapons are becoming more affordable. For Australia, it is the quality of the people in the ADF that will provide our edge: the people who develop the systems, the people who train the operators and the people who operate the weapons. People are the critical resource.

But the quality of our individual people is only the start. Everyone knows an example of a team of 'ordinary' players beating talented individuals not playing as a team. The vital component of a team is leadership – leadership can make ordinary Australians do extraordinary things. Leadership is not just another specialist competency to be learned like logistics or fiscal management; rather, it is the key to unlock the potential of our people. Economists refer to a 'multiplier effect' when one change has a cascading effect out of all proportion to the original change. Leadership is the 'multiplier' to give the ADF the capability edge into the 21st Century.

Australia's Defence White Paper (*Defence 2000*) focuses on the importance of leadership. To ensure success in military operations and foster a first-class work environment, Defence must have effective leaders at all levels. Good leaders focus their efforts on supporting their people, and on building up commitment, skills and teamwork to achieve results. The day to day behaviour of senior leaders, both civilian and military, can either support or undermine attempts to make Defence a more rewarding place to work.

The ADF has consistently demonstrated the quality of its leadership in military operations, particularly at the tactical level. However, new leadership challenges have emerged. These include a mixed military, civilian and commercial workforce and a greater emphasis on ensuring Defence resources are used efficiently, as well as effectively.

Not surprisingly, Defence is implementing a range of senior leadership development initiatives. Over the next few years, these initiatives will be embedded in personnel policies, and education and training systems. The aim is to ensure that an effective 'leadership culture' is in place, as opposed to a 'bureaucratic culture'. Improving leadership will remain one of Defence's highest priorities.

The Evolution of the Centre for Defence Leadership Studies

With the development of the Australian Defence College concept in the late 1990s, there was a realisation that effort needed to be placed into leadership development at the new institution and more generally across the Australian Defence Force. This process was not the result of any organisational leadership failure, but rather because of the recognition that the world was changing fast, that much work was underway in leadership research and that with Australia's commitment to securing peace and independence for in East Timor, the nation's tempo of military activity was on the increase. The Defence White Paper in 2000 stressed that improving leadership would be one of Defence's highest priorities.

The Secretary of the Department of Defence, Dr. Allan Hawke, in 2001, also stressed the value of leadership development occurring in a continuum as part of professional military education for Defence personnel at the Australian Defence Force Academy, the Australian Command and Staff Course and the Centre for Defence and Strategic Studies. At the same time the Chief of the Defence Force and the Secretary (the diarchy) were embedding an organisational renewal process across Defence. The Secretary saw the evolving leadership centre as a major player in shaping this developmental progression.

The Army had already established a Centre for Command Studies at the Staff College at Queenscliff in Victoria in 1997. Its task was "to develop, promote and implement command leadership and management education and training for Army leaders." The Centre had a staff of five - four military and one civilian, and its initial areas of activity included developing competencies for the command, leadership and management education and training continuum across all ranks; conduct of a risk management training analysis review for the Army; writing leadership doctrine; and developing an Army Leadership Model. The Centre was productive, and prior to its disbandment in 1998, as part of a Defence effort to save manpower, had developed both a solid reputation and a wide network.

The increased emphasis on leadership was also evident in the Commissioning letter for the new Commander of the Australian Defence College. Issued in September 2000, it stated that the ADC is "now, and will increasingly be, a centre of expertise……Improved leadership and strategic management abilities will increasingly be in demand in an international and national security context marked by high levels of complexity and risk." It continued, "Defence and other agencies need people who are well prepared to provide sound policy options, lead in uncertain and complex situations and manage security into the future." The letter further highlighted the Commander's accountability for "the corporate development of a strong centre of expertise on command and leadership, with an associated active program to support command and leadership development in and beyond the Australian Defence College." The direction to the new commander also stated, "You should work with recognised centres of expertise, including Headquarters Australian Theatre (now Joint Operations Command), the Australian Defence Force Warfare Centre and the Australian Public Service Merit Protection Commission, to identify and help Defence achieve best practice."

The new institution was able to utilise position savings from the amalgamation of the three Service staff colleges to establish a small leadership centre of expertise. During the development of the operating concept for the Centre in 2001, the following Defence definitions for its activities were used:

Command. Command is the lawful authority that an individual in the Services exerts over subordinates by virtue of his or her rank or appointment. The exercise of command is supported by the existence of a code of military law.

Leadership. Leadership is the ability of an individual to influence others effectively in a given situation, based on a combination of that individual's knowledge, skills and attitudes.

Management. Management involves those continuing actions of planning, organising, directing, coordinating, controlling and evaluating the use of people, money, materials and facilities to accomplish an activity or task.

Development. Development entails positive changes in an individual towards mastery of a knowledge or skill, through formal and informal education, training, work experience, secondments, coaching and mentoring.

The Centre for Defence Command Leadership and Management Studies (CDCLMS) was established at the Australian Defence College (ADC) Weston Creek campus in January 2002. Three years later, it was renamed the Centre for Defence Leadership Studies (CDLS). The senior leadership recognised that much good work was already underway in the broader Defence community on command, leadership and management activities, but that the work tended to occur in isolation. Rather than direct, or duplicate, these activities, the aim of the Centre was to act as a central Defence point of contact providing a framework for sharing information, tabling concepts, and assisting with such activities. As such, the role of the Centre is to provide the Commander ADC, with corporate-level command, leadership and management development advice in order to help shape expertise in these areas in the College and across Defence in general.

The functions of the Centre are to:

- Provide Commander ADC with specialist advice to ensure command, leadership and management development activities sponsored by the ADC are conducted effectively and efficiently;
- Provide a strategic-level framework to allow Defence individuals and groups involved in command, leadership and management development activities to share information and ideas;
- Conduct research on command, leadership and management issues of interest to Defence and produce papers and articles;
- Support those command, leadership and management development activities referred to the Centre by Defence groups by providing advice on more appropriate, effective or efficient skills and strategies; and
- Build and share a comprehensive body of professional knowledge on command, leadership and management issues.

In 2006, the Centre had a staff of three (two civilians and one military officer), as well as a small group of visiting fellows, who are engaged on specific tasks on a part-time basis. Although it reports to the Commander of the Australian Defence College, who carries the rank of a two-star general, it is often tasked by, and has access to, the Chief of the Defence Force and the Service Chiefs.

The Centre's mission is "to shape the development of commanders, leaders and managers across Defence who can ethically win today and tomorrow." Moreover, its vision is stated to be "excellence for Defence in command, leadership and management."

The Centre operates as a think-tank and due to its limited human resources and small budget, relies heavily on its national and international networks to conduct environmental scans and access the latest research. The Centre's three member staff all have Masters of Arts degrees. However, the Centre also relies on the specialists with PhDs in its group of Visiting Fellows to assist with research and conceptual work. The Centre has had since its inception, a very clear operational focus and its work supports the practitioner leaders at all levels of Defence. It is also important to note that the Centre has done practical work in supporting command developments, particularly following the 2003 Iraq war.

In 2002, the Centre developed a model that outlined the Defence approach to leadership development and it remains a fluid canvas with the latest development being the one and two-star generals' course in recognition of the operating tempo and the requirement to 'top up' the command and leadership skills of defence's strategic leaders. It is given in Figure 1.

Within the Australian Defence College a leadership development continuum continues to evolve. It is shown in Figure 2.

Australian Character

Leadership is all about character. It is about you. In this respect, it is important to have an understanding of where Australians are coming from, particularly in a discourse about how nations are developing their military leaders. Professor David Horner provides an interesting perspective on Australian character in his seminal work on command titled, "Towards a Philosophy of Australian Command," and it is captured in full in this extract:

> *The nature and character of the Australian people, and specifically of the Australian serviceman, is the most elusive factor to quantify. The Australian soldiers at*

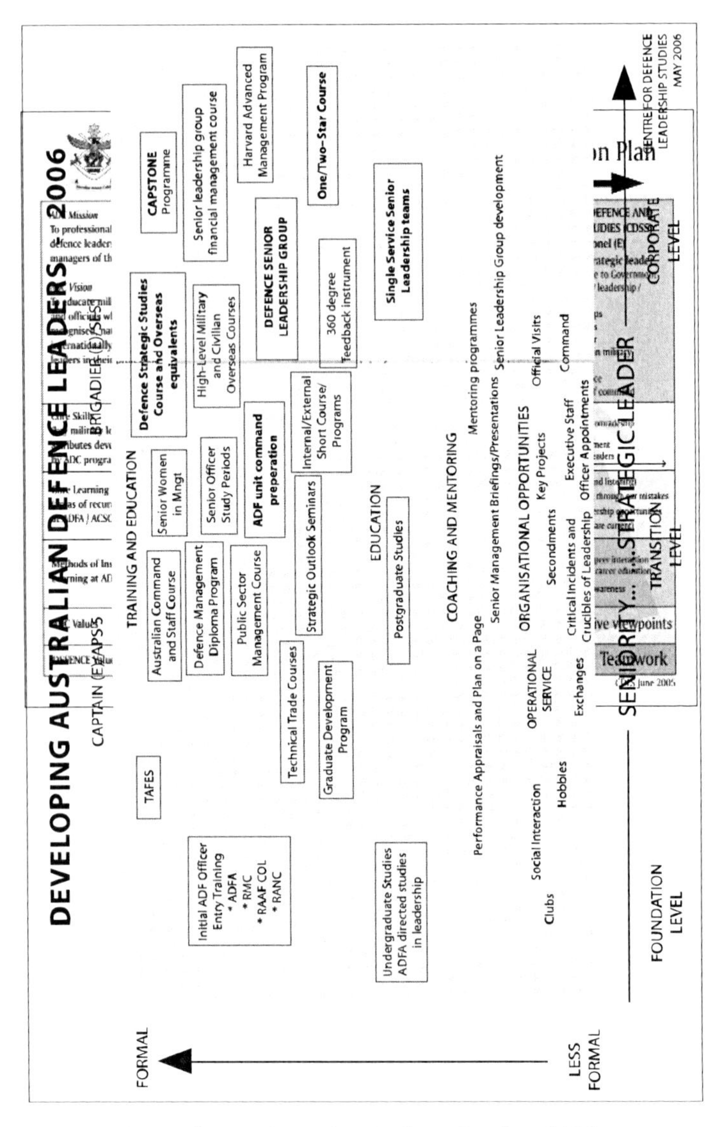

FIGURE 1: Developing Australian Defence Leaders 2006

Australian Defence College Leadership Education Plan

TRANSACTIONAL/TRANSFORMATIONAL (at all stages)

ADC Mission To professionally educate defence leaders and managers of the future **ADC Vision** To educate military officers and officials who are recognised, nationally and internationally, as world leaders in their profession	**AUSTRALIAN DEFENCE FORCE ACADEMY (ADFA)** **The junior tactical leader** • foundation knowledge, skills, attitudes • situational leadership • effective teamwork • 'joint mates' • personal leadership • member of a unit	**AUSTRALIAN COMMAND AND STAFF COLLEGE (ASCS)** **The Major (E) tactical/ operational leader** • unit command perspectives • good governance framework • joint working relationships • plan joint operations • management competence (operations, resource, risk, change, information) • whole of government approach • operational ethics • foundations for strategic leadership	**CENTRE FOR DEFENCE AND STRATEGIC STUDIES (CDSS)** **The Colonel (E) operational/strategic leader** • provide policy advice to Govt. • strategic command/leadership/ management • strategic relationships • plan joint comapigns • apply military power • develop and maintain military capability • corporate governance • ethical dimension of command
Core Skills (key military leadership attributes developed by ADC programs)	• inter-personal skills/working in multi-disciplinary teams • technical excellence • networking • business planning/resource management • problem solving/decision making • JMAP • comradeship • framework of ethical values • leading across cultures • motivation for self improvement • emotional intelligence • cultural intelligence • policy facilitators/leaders • personal fitness		
Core Learning Areas (areas of recurring focus at ADFA/ACSC and CDSS)	• Australian society/agencies/process (context of ADO leadership) • communication (oral, written and listening) • leadership theory • ADO perspective/structures/processes (mechanics of ADO leadership) • external evaluation • Australian military history (as a vehicle for leadership lessons) • learning through our mistakes • extra-curricular leadership opportunities • ethical decision making (confirming Defence values) • comtemporary operational context (ensure lessons are current)		
Methods of Instruction/ Learning at ADC	• individual research • case studies • comprehensive, coordinated educational approach • practical leadership exercises/experiential learning/field activity • syndicate work/peer interaction • mentoring • 360-degree feedback tools • lectures • through career education • self-awareness		
ADC Values	**Academic integrity Innovation Research Intellectual debate Alternative viewpoints**		
DEFENCE Values	**Professionalism Loyalty Innovation Courage Integrity Teamwork**		

FIGURE 2: Australian Defence College Leadership Education Plan

Gallipoli, and more generally during the First World War, were seen as reflecting the character of the Australian people. Although the 'Anzac spirit' has its origins in the achievements of Australian citizen soldiers at Gallipoli, it has been absorbed and adopted by all three Australian Services, including the regular forces. The official historian, Charles Bean, argued that the First World War diggers exemplified qualities of self-reliance and mateship that had been developed from living in the Australian bush. Facing fire, drought and flood, they had learned that survival demanded cooperation and helping one's mates. They had also learned to live without the creature comforts of city life.

Historians have pointed out that the majority of soldiers in the First World War actually came from the cities. But the proponents of the 'bush ethos' have claimed that city folk before the First World War usually had a strong connection with the country. Indeed, it has been argued that even into the latter part of the twentieth century Australians were outdoors people who relished an opportunity to get out of the city. Writing in 1979, an Australian Army major with service in Vietnam, claimed that in his experience "even one or two 'country boys' exert a disproportionate effect on a group (of soldiers) relative to their number in that group." Whether it was based on the bush ethos, there is no doubt that mateship became a dominant characteristic of the Australian Services.

Linked to mateship was the concept of equality. In the early twentieth century, Australia was a far more egalitarian society than Britain, with its class structure, and this carried over into the Army. The officer corps generally consisted of men with higher levels of education, but included some with only moderate education who had been promoted because of abilities displayed in battle. Soldiers had little respect for rank, status and class, and readily followed officers who were good leaders and capable soldiers. As many officers had come from the ranks, they empathised with their soldiers and exercised care and responsibility for them. Australian soldiers were quick to detect if their commanders were selfishly pursuing their own advancement. Perhaps unfairly, the men of the 5th Australian Division in 1916 thought that their commander, Major-General James McCay, was seeking personal advancement and lost confidence in him. Successful Australian commanders put the needs of their men before personal advancement. They understood the irreverence and humour of the ordinary Australian soldiers and built upon these character traits in establishing rapport with them.

Coming from a democratic society, the soldiers had a heightened sense of justice, or an expectation that everyone would receive a 'fair go'. They were civilians who had volunteered for war service, rather than regular soldiers, and thus the diggers saw little need for parade-ground discipline, even though they recognised the necessity for discipline in battle.

Historians and scholars have argued that the commanders of the First Australian Imperial Force (AIF) who exercised control over these men developed a particularly Australian approach to command. They did not see themselves a socially superior to their men, they understood the imperative of giving everyone a 'fair go', and they saw the soldiers as their mates. More detailed research of life in the First AIF, however, has suggested that this stereotype is not necessarily valid. There were often tensions between the officers and the men. Some officers were appointed because of their social position. And Australian officers could also be sticklers for discipline. Nonetheless, just as Australian soldiers were different from British soldiers, so too, Australian officers were different.

In the Second World War, soldiers who were commissioned after attending officer training schools did not usually return to their previous units. They were therefore less likely to look upon their soldiers as their mates. But in the main, the other characteristics persisted. Indeed the soldiers of the Second AIF consciously assumed the responsibility of maintaining the ANZAC legend established by their fathers twenty years earlier.

The formation of the Regular Army after the Second World War changed the ethos further. The soldiers retained the concepts of mateship and a fair go, but there was less equality. Officers still came from all walks of life, but they were trained at officer schools for lengthy periods and most had not served in the ranks. The Regular soldiers spent more time in peacetime training than on operations and a high level of discipline was demanded of them.These developments probably brought changes to the Australian approach to command.

Changing norms in society in the late twentieth century brought further developments in the nature and character of the Australian people. Society became more multi-cultural, self-centred and materialistic. Better-educated young service people demanded explanations from their commanders, not simple orders. Commanders were faced with the problems of integrating women into combat and support units that had previously been the preserve of males. Many combat support functions were taken over by civilian contractors who were not subject to military 'command'. The increasing emphasis in the community on the rights of individuals led to a greater willingness to resolve matters by resorting to litigation, and commanders increasingly had to worry about administrative law as they commanded their units. Commanders had to expect that their actions might be subject to the scrutiny of the media, and in turn they would be appraised by a sceptical society that might have little sympathy for the military ethos.

Despite these changes in society, the old character traits of mateship, egalitarianism, irreverence, humour, and lack of respect for rank and status are still evident in the ADF and are reflected in command relationships. The ANZAC legend is alive and well in the ADF, giving it a distinct approach to command and more broadly to military service.

Only the Australian Army has attempted to give its officers any guidance as to the qualities that might be needed in a commander (i.e. leadership, robustness, courage and resolution, boldness, professional knowledge, judgement, decisiveness and flexibility, integrity, and creative imagination), and has endorsed the broad philosophy of command - directive control. However, the identification of the list qualities should not be just an academic exercise: training and education programs should be designed to develop these qualities. Similarly, command structures should be designed to allow for directive control, and commanders should be educated about it.

If it is assumed that these command qualities and the philosophy of directive control (mission command) are broadly applicable to Western defence forces, the question remains as to whether there are specific characteristics of Australian command that have survived the societal and organisational changes of the late twentieth century. As such, the following is a list of possible characteristics. Australian commanders:

- expect to operate in a joint-Service environment, and are comfortable with it;
- have long experience of operating within a coalition and understand the ambiguities of reporting to an Allied force commander while watching out for Australian national interests and retaining their responsibility to the Australian government;
- are keenly aware that they draw their authority from the Australian government and, through it, from the Australian people;
- are extremely careful to preserve Australian lives but understand that in certain circumstances lives must be risked to achieve desired military outcomes;
- operate under the rule of law, conscious of the Laws of Armed Conflict and of Australian national law, and apply military discipline in accordance with the Defence Force Disciplinary Act;
- are flexible and ready to improvise to achieve desired outcomes, even though adequate resources might not be available;
- operate through cooperation in dealing with other commanders rather than by slavishly following formal command structures;
- display an egalitarian approach with their subordinates, leading by example and conscious of giving every one a 'fair go';

- are concerned for the welfare of their subordinates and put the good of the unit before their own advancement;
- are compassionate and humane in dealing with civilians, refugees, displaced persons etc;
- understand and appreciate the Australian sense of humour, with its lack of reverence for rank and status; and,
- are professionally competent.

This discussion has brought to light possible shortcomings in the ADF's approach to command. The ADF needs to do more work in articulating the general qualities that are thought desirable in a commander and in ensuring that these qualities are developed through training and education. Professor Horner's work is used extensively in the professional military education environment in Australia.

The Development of Strategic Leaders

Defence conducts an annual internal attitudes survey and the process regularly focuses on the performance of senior leaders in the organisation. In 2004, a segment of the results were shown on this chart:

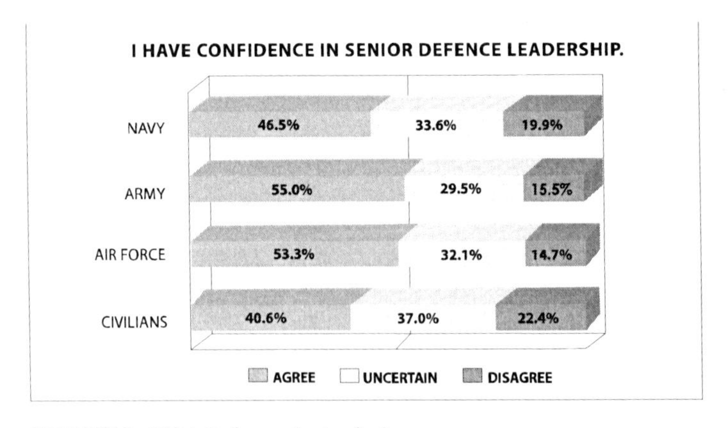

FIGURE 3: 2004 Defence Attitude Survey

The Capstone Program

Senior leadership realized that more work needed to be done in developing senior leaders. The Capstone program, which focuses on building the capacity of participants to perform as members of Defence's Senior Leadership Group (SLG), has been delivered since 2001, and has undergone progressive refinement. Stakeholder and participant evaluation of Capstone's structure and outcomes indicate that the design strategy is sound. In essence, the Capstone program aims to help new members to contribute effectively as part of the Defence SLG.

The Secretary, Chief of the Defence Force and Defence Committee (DC) have an active involvement and interest in raising awareness of the practical issues currently facing the senior leadership and putting into perspective the strategic priorities that shape Defence's relationship with government and actively participate throughout the program.
The DC has strong ideas about the outcomes it requires from the Capstone program; this means that some elements of the Capstone design are not discretionary.

Defence leaders, whether participants, mentors, managers or peers are expected, through their contact with the Capstone program to:

- Foster and achieve closer alignment with organisational goals and provide more cohesive support for organisational intent;
- Identify and develop ways of working at the strategic level that recognise and respond to the challenges of complexity and diversity across Defence; and,
- Develop and deploy the Defence Leadership Model in ways that recognise and support behaviour congruent with Defence values.

Capstone aims to:

- Build and exercise strategic leadership skills;
- Develop a style for working with and leading others that is strategic, consistent with individual preferences and Defence values;
- Integrate strategic leadership roles within Defence's organisational, business management and decision processes;
- Ensure that strategic leadership behaviour has measurable consequences that contribute to Defence's capacity to achieve its mission and sustain continuing organisational improvement; and,
- Assist all members of the SLG to contribute effectively to the Defence outcome.

The heart of the Capstone process is conducted as a five-day Residential experience. At an individual level, Capstone also provides an opportunity for each participant to reflect on their own leadership experience and attributes and to do so in the context of the strategic issues and challenges facing Defence. Reflection can often provide impetus for moving forward and identifying new leadership development challenges and goals.

Once were Warriors?

Strategic leadership is a fascinating area of research in any organisation but in Defence the ramifications of decisions made by strategic leaders are arguably more serious. In 2002 and 2003, Dr. Nick Jans and Dr. Jane Harte, under the sponsorship of the Chief of the Army, conducted research on the organisational culture of the Australian Defence Force. The results of the study were published in December 2003 under the intriguing title *Once were warriors? Leadership, culture and organisational change in the Australian Defence Organisation* and the further development of this work is sponsored by the Australian Defence College. The authors argued, "having the right leaders is not the same as having the right leadership. If innovation in Defence is often tortuous and inconclusive, this is not because its leaders lack skill and intelligence or because they are 'conservative." (Besides, most – in the current generation anyway – are not.) Rather,

CENTRAL ELEMENTS OF CAPSTONE

CAPSTONE'S STRATEGIC FOCUS

DC-driven
Reality based
Consciousness raising
Values based
Strategy connected
Leadership capability linked

DEFENCE VALUES "PLICIT"[2]

Professionalism
Loyalty
Integrity
Courage
Innovation
Teamwork

CAPSTONE'S AIMS

- Practicing leadership that reflects the five leadership capabilities
- Ensuring Defence values underpin all behaviour in Defence
- Stimulating strategic thinking, discussion and innovation
- Valuing being part of the Senior Leadership Group
- Promoting a Defence-wide perspective when working in Defence

SENIOR LEADERSHIP CAPABILITIES AND LINKAGES

Set the standard for performance	Performance beyond the ordinary
Give meaningful direction	Control the business
Make communication a priority	Feedback on communication
Create the climate for success	Choices that leaders make
Persist until the job is well and truly done	Make a difference

DEFENCE STRATEGIC THEMES

- Developing the capability to win today and tomorrow
- Creating the climate where people do their best
- Promoting quality advice and decision-making
- Getting best value from the Defence dollar
- Making the best use of science and technology and Australian industry
- Strangthening international relationships for Australian's security

FIGURE 4: CENTRAL ELEMENTS OF CAPSTONE

[2] PLICIT = professionalism, loyalty, integrity, courage, innovation and teamwork.

it is because of the way that organisational practices inadvertently constrain the pace of change by promoting a short-term and incremental approach to strategic problem solving. Three long – established staffing practices in particular – senior officer churn, staff officer churn, and a generalist model of career development – act as an 'iron triangle' that perpetuates Defence's 'bureaucratic culture'. These policies, designed to ensure the dominance of the warrior ethos in Defence, have the inadvertent consequence of constraining officers' opportunities to develop any substantial professional expertise outside this role. 'Warriors' they were and, for the majority, 'warriors' they remain. The dominance of a warrior ethos at junior and middle levels is an unequivocal strength for the Organisation, but a mixed blessing at the top.' The study focused on the churn issue, highlighting that the time in the job for senior military leaders in Defence averaged 1.2 years and that of civilian executives in defence, 1.9 years. It also tackled the issues of tribalism, jointery, the military profession in Australia and leadership culture.

Few other Western militaries appear to have taken such an intimate snapshot of their strategic leadership culture and the results are important because the methodology was to interview and record the perspectives of present and retired strategic leaders. The study continues to be discussed in detail by the senior leaders of Defence and is directed reading at the Staff College.

A Joint Approach To Leadership Development Through Performance Appraisals

A leadership development advantage of the ADF is that common annual performance appraisals are used for all ADF Officers and Senior Non - Commissioned Officers (Sr NCO). There is a common language for leadership assessment each year and the focus is leading others to achieve a productive, efficient, skilled, motivated and cohesive workforce. The assessment aspires to develop leaders who can perform in highly complex and demanding circumstances.

Education in Leadership and Military Ethics

When planning for a year - plant corn; when planning for a decade - plant trees; when planning for life - train and educate people.[3] This is the theme of the Australian Defence College strategic plan. Important to this theme is the teaching of ethics, which is simply a set of principles or standards, by which your actions may be judged good or bad, right or wrong. Military ethics is simply the application of ethics to military endeavours.

In June 2005, the Australian Senate reported that a decade of rolling inquiries had not met with the broad-based change required to protect the rights of Service personnel. This failure to expose such abuse means the system stumbles at its most elementary stage – the reporting of wrongdoing. Complaints were made to these inquiries about recent events including suicides, deaths through accident, major illicit drug use, serious abuses of power in training schools and cadet units, flawed prosecutions and failed, poor investigations.

Ethical failures have occurred in Western militaries over the past few decades, and they continue in the 21st Century. The failures, noted one scholar, "have involved military and public service personnel of all age groups, all elements and without regard to religion, ethnicity, gender or any other criteria."

This extends to deployments. Combat operations inevitably involve death and destruction. Nevertheless, all ADF members need to adhere to the Law of Armed Conflict and the moral principles that underlie them, so that military operations are conducted in ways that ensure the ADF retains its legitimacy as a fighting force.

In recent times, there have been suggestions that some serious operational incidents have highlighted ethical problems[4]

[3] Guanzi, c 645 BC. Quoted in the *Australian Defence College Strategic Plan 2005-2015*.

[4] For instance the 1996 Australian Army Black Hawk disaster.

and that the ADF's operational tempo will continue to see the nation involved in operations well beyond Australia, where we will continue to operate independently or as part of a coalition and Australians will be in command. The fact that Australian forces have performed to a high ethical standard in the past can be attributed to the quality of leadership, training and a degree of luck. However, the Senate report on the effectiveness of Australia's military justice system tabled on 16 June 2005 highlighted areas of concern that need to be addressed in the professional military educational environment. The volatility, uncertainty, complexity and ambiguity of our operating environment suggests we need to prepare our leaders for the challenges of the future by educating them in the ethical issues that have emerged in recent conflicts, deployments and garrison incidents. We can no longer afford to be reactive in this regard.

At the Australian Defence Force Ethics Seminar in July 2002, the first of its kind, the participants agreed that more effort needed to be put into education in military ethics in the ADF. The Seminar agreed that the Centre for Defence Leadership Studies be allocated the development responsibility.

Over the past decade, the nature of ADF operational experience has raised ethical dilemmas for Australian commanders and personnel, and the challenges in Rwanda, East Timor, Afghanistan and Iraq immediately come to mind. There was also extensive commentary in the media about the ADF's ethical challenges in the "Children Overboard Affair" in 2001 and it continued into 2006. The operational experience of the Canadian Forces in Somalia in 1993 highlighted serious ethical failures that the Canadians continue to address through sophisticated educational programmes. In the United States, all services operate military ethics programmes. Until 2003, little was being done on a holistic basis in the ADF beyond the *ab initio* education at the Australian Defence Force Academy and the Service colleges. Pilot military ethics programmes were delivered to Staff College and the Strategic Studies Course in 2003 and the programmes evolved following comprehensive student feedback. In 2005, the Staff College course gave positive feedback to the programme. What has become clear is that students want to spend more time discussing ethical issues in the military profession.

The Australian Defence College programs, conducted as two-day workshops, use some of the principles suggested by the Harvard Business School:

- *Ethics is as much an attitude as it is a set of skills and knowledge;*

- *Outstanding leaders, organisations, and practice are emphasized;*

- *The focus is on decision making with all its complexity and ambiguity, not on issues of ethics or social responsibility in isolation; and,*

- *Early instruction is important to allow course members to reflect on issues throughout the year.*

The programmes use the Defence Values of *professionalism*, *loyalty*, *innovation*, *courage*, *integrity* and *teamwork* as the basis for discussion and have an operational focus. They contribute to the development of operational and strategic leaders by:

- Recognition of the centrality of ethical values in the context of individual and organisational effectiveness and national support of the ADF;

- Recognition of the breadth of responsibility of the modern military, as well as the constraints and trade-offs attending the exercise of that responsibility; and,

- Encouragement of reflection on the value and constraints in the course members own approach to military ethics.

The programs focus on Australian defence experiences and topics covered include two fascinating historical perspectives. The first is about Lieutenant Harry 'the Breaker' Morant who was found guilty of murdering prisoners in the Boer War and was executed by firing squad. Over the years in print and on film, Morant was portrayed as a hero and scapegoat for British military failures. More recently military historians have labelled him a serial killer.

The second case covers the actions of Major-General Gordon Bennett who left his 8th Division as they went into Japanese captivity at Changi POW camp in Singapore in 1942. His actions still generate debate to this day. Some regard him as a villain and a coward whilst veterans remain loyal to his memory to this day.

In 2006, for the first time in many years and in part due to stories emerging from the 'long war', the Australian Command and Staff College revisited the moral issues surrounding the My Lai massacre. Contemporary case studies include the 1994-95 ADF Rwanda experience, where ADF personnel were placed in the most horrific situations imaginable; the 1996 Black Hawk disaster which killed 18 personnel and generated many command and leadership questions; Operation Allied Force in the Balkans in 1999 which examines the legality or otherwise of the NATO air campaign in the Balkans; the loss of four lives in the HMAS *Westralia* fire in 1998 which revealed systemic failures in the Navy; the 2001 children overboard affair where the chain of command and communication broke down during the Federal election period; the Air Force F-111 fuel tank deseal / reseal catastrophe where over a period of 20 years personnel were exposed to toxic chemicals; and, the Canadian experience in Somalia in 1993.

In 2006, the programme included study of the Senate report on the effectiveness of Australia's military justice system. Two years earlier, in 2004, the Centre also delivered elements of their military ethics programme to the Singapore Armed Forces.

The philosophical approach, as described by Dr. Simon Longstaff, that the Centre has adhered to is that "the truth about ethics and the human condition is that there is no prescriptive answer. It is judgemental and there are no assurances of certainty." With this in mind, the presenters of the ethical case studies offer little in the way of solutions but a great deal of material for reflection. Workshops include sessions on ethical intelligence and 'dirty hands' theory, which argues that the further you go up in an organisation the more you are likely to be faced with getting your hands dirty.

Another critical part of the workshop process is the active participation of the student bodies with their unparalleled collective experience. As such, the power of the presentations are reinforced by the participation of individuals involved in the incidents under discussion. Education in the sphere of military ethics is a key component of the Australian Defence College focus on achieving the necessary balance of 'how to think' and 'what to think' in helping Australian leaders acquire a competitive edge.

The Development Of The ADF Joint Leadership Doctrine

The Australian Army first published formal leadership doctrine in 1973. Since then, the original publication has been updated on at least two occasions, the last being in 2002. Nevertheless, both the Royal Australian Navy (RAN) and Royal Australian Air Force (RAAF) were content to develop their leaders in the absence of any formal leadership doctrine. With the advent of the Australian Defence Force Academy in 1986 and then the joint Australian Command and Staff Course in 2001, this dearth of leadership doctrine from the Navy and Air Force meant that the Army's "Land Warfare Doctrine - Leadership" became the de facto leadership doctrine for these tri-service institutions. Not surprisingly, some elements within the Navy and RAAF were not entirely happy with this situation. In 2005, the Joint Doctrine Steering Group tasked ADC to produce Joint Leadership Doctrine for the ADF.

Inspired by the very good publication *Leadership in the Canadian Forces: Doctrine* and its sister publication *Leadership in the Canadian Forces: Conceptual Foundations,*[5] both published in 2005, the Centre for Defence Leadership Studies set out to produce Joint Leadership Doctrine (JLD) for the ADF. Currently, the JLD is before the Joint Doctrine Steering Group in draft format. The draft publication represents a departure from the Australian Army's publications on leadership in that it starts with the conceptual foundations for leadership and finishes with descriptions of how the ADF develops its leaders. Many of the ideas and concepts for the draft JLD were unashamedly borrowed from the Canadian documents mentioned above, mainly because they were seen to represent "best practice" in respect to military leadership conceptual foundations and doctrine. Much like the Canadian publications, the draft JLD commences with a workable definition of leadership and then builds logically from this point to construct the values-based approach to leadership, an approach used by both the ADF and the Canadian Forces.

In Chapter 1, the draft JLD describes the process of leadership as it would be observed anywhere. This "description of process" is far from exhaustive, but it outlines the essential components of any leadership relationship. The draft JLD builds on this foundation in Chapter 2 by describing the differences between leadership in the military and leadership in civilian society. Importantly, these differences are in addition to the components already identified – they are not replacements. The draft publication then moves to leadership in the ADF and describes the two leadership functions of "leading people" in Chapter 3 and "leading the organisation" in Chapter 4. Both titles are similar to those that appear in the Canadian doctrine! Predictably, these functions share much with leadership in other militaries. The differences, and there

[5] Canada, *Leadership in the Canadian Forces: Conceptual Foundations* (Kingston: DND, 2005) and Canada, *Leadership in the Canadian Forces: Doctrine* (Kingston: DND, 2005) are available at www.cda-acd.forces.gc.ca/cfli/

are some stark ones, generally highlight the different cultures rather than suggest that leadership in the ADF is somehow unusual or unique. As would be expected with such a popular concept, leadership in the ADF has far more in common with other organisations and militaries than it has in variance.

Certain themes and principles thread through most chapters of the draft JLD. The exception is Chapter 5, in which some controversial leadership issues are introduced. Cultural alignment, gender and diversity in the ADF are examined, along with some dysfunctional leadership behaviours that can surface within any military.

Much like leadership itself, the draft JLD sets out to influence members to adopt desired values, principles and behaviours by showing a logical connection between leadership and the ADF's mission. Although a description of strategic-level leadership is given, the guidance within the draft JLD focuses upon the operational-level issues of leadership in the ADF. Chapter 6 brings this focus into sharp contrast by discussing and describing the development of ADF leaders up to the lieutenant-colonel level. This is not to say, however, that there is nothing in the publication for senior officers and their staff. Most militaries recognise that leadership development of the next generation is a strategic leader responsibility and that continued review and reflection upon the material in the draft publication will ensure its ongoing relevance. The material immediately below is extracted from the draft Doctrine.

Values

Values are beliefs about what is considered centrally important in life. Values guide people's thoughts, decisions, behaviours and interactions. In the Australian context, the Federal Government has identified nine values that are taught in Australian schools (i.e. Care and Compassion, Doing Your Best, Fair Go, Freedom, Honesty and Trustworthiness, Integrity, Respect, Responsibility and lastly, Understanding, Tolerance and Inclusion.)

The Government believes that encouraging its future adult citizens to adopt and live by such values will lead to a more cohesive and purposeful society. In a sense, the Government is outlining an ethical framework that will help guide individuals to assess the difference between right and wrong.

Trustworthiness

Trustworthiness is one Australian value or trait that deserves special attention. Much has been written on leadership traits such as self-confidence, intelligence and adaptability. Most of these are internal to the leader and are hard to observe from the follower perspective. Trustworthiness, on the other hand, is a trait that will be quickly assessed by followers and, for that reason alone, is perhaps the most import leadership character trait. Trust in leadership is positively related to individual and group performance, persistence in the face of adversity and the ability to withstand stress. A climate of trust between leaders and the led is also positively related to such qualities as conscientiousness, fair play and co-operation.

Organisational Values.

Organisations within Australia identify values that they believe will lead to behaviours that will benefit the organisation's purpose or aspirations. Australian organisations see values like 'innovation' and 'adaptability' as important because they believe values like these guide behaviour to a desirable end-state. Values are not seen by organisations as replacements for rules but hopefully values act alongside rules as 'correct-path-beacons' in foggy situations where the strict application of rules is not obvious. Much has been written about 'organisational values' and the importance of aligning an individual's values with those of the organisation.

Although few organisations would object to the nine values taught in Australian schools, organisations tend to espouse values with a stronger business focus. The leadership aspect to this notion has two related elements. Firstly, a leader cannot reasonably espouse organisation values and then be seen to operate by a different (or opposing) set of values. Put simply, a leader is immediately compromised if he/she espouses "honesty" in business and is then caught being untruthful to a client. Secondly, all leaders within an organisation have a role to play in aligning the values of members with the values espoused by the organisation. If the values of the members do not align with the values of the organisation, then dissonance will result between the member and the organisation, resulting in less than optimum performance from both.

Typical Military Values

Military forces tend to espouse values that are relevant to war fighting and therefore more demanding than those of civilian organisations. Society recognises that the 'operational imperative' is sufficient grounds to espouse values that would hold less weight in society at large. Values such as honour, duty, selfless commitment, courage, discipline and loyalty are more prevalent in military organisations than in wider society (where some of these concepts are less well understood). These professional military values are concepts derived from the demands of battle. Battlefield situations induce tremendous fear and confusion in individuals. It is no surprise that courage is valued so highly in the military environment since it is courage that is the foil of fear. If someone displays ample courage then the process of influencing them to willingly go into battle is so much easier than if, say, they were imbued with values pertaining to self-preservation.

Australian Defence Force Values

The ADF subscribes to a set of six values: professionalism, loyalty, integrity, courage, innovation and teamwork. This set of values, which goes by the acronym "PLICIT," resonates well with the value sets of the three single Services. The single Service values reflect the uniqueness of the separate Services and they compliment and expand the Defence values.

The ADF has amplified each of the PLICIT values so that they provide better guidance in regard to expected behaviour. These amplification statements are listed below:

Professionalism is striving for excellence in everything we do. In Defence we will work hard to deliver high quality results, do our job to the best of our ability and take pride in our achievements. We will be sensitive to changes in our working environment and ready to respond. We will provide impartial, comprehensive, timely and accurate advice. We will constantly seek to improve our work performance.

Loyalty is being committed to each other and to Defence. In Defence we will serve the Government of the day and support our leaders and colleagues to undertake tasks and achieve results in line with Government direction. We will treat everyone at all levels with respect, care and compassion. We will work to uphold the best interests of the Australian people.

Integrity is behaving honestly and ethically, and demonstrating the highest standards of probity in our personal conduct. We will act fairly and accept personal responsibility for our decisions and actions. We will build trust through productive working relationships. We will not allow the fine Australian traditions of mateship to be misused to cover up bad behaviour or bring the organisation into disrepute. Our actions will clearly match our words.

Courage is the strength of character to honor our convictions (moral *courage*) and bravery in the face of personal harm (physical *courage*). In Defence we will stand up for what we believe is right and we will speak out robustly and openly against what is wrong. We will have the *courage* to accept valid criticism to admit to errors, learn lessons and improve. We will give honest feedback on work performance.

Innovation is actively looking for better ways of doing business. In Defence we will be open to new ideas and strive to identify and implement better ways of doing business. We will be clever and make best use of the resources that we have to do our job. We will encourage sensible risk taking, and strive to identify opportunities to eliminate inefficiency and waste.

Teamwork is working together with respect, trust and collective purpose. *Teamwork* is cultivated through strong, positive leadership and attention to the needs of team members. In Defence *teamwork* is integral to everything we do, and will characterise our working relationships inside Defence and across the whole of Government. We will foster collaborative workplaces, communicate openly and solve problems in a collegiate manner, share ideas and take advantage of the diversity of our knowledge and experience.

ANECDOTES

Chief Petty Officer "Buck" Rogers was a living example of ADF values. On the last night of "Buck's" life, the aircraft carrier HMAS *Melbourne* and the destroyer HMAS *Voyager* were conducting exercises off the New South Wales south coast. In the late evening, *Voyager* crossed in front of *Melbourne* and the two ships collided, with *Melbourne* smashing the destroyer in half. Rogers was one of more than 50 men trapped in darkness in a compartment of the sinking forward section. He took control and tried to bring calm in the disastrous situation. He probably realised that not all would be able to get through a small escape hatch and that he, being a large man, had no chance at all. "He was more intent on getting the younger chaps out first," said a survivor. The forward section finally sank about ten minutes after the impact. Rogers was heard leading his remaining doomed comrades in a prayer and a hymn during their final moments.

Possibly the best known Australian soldier during the Second World War, Lieutenant "Diver" Derrick was seen by many as the embodiment of all those best characteristics widely attributed to the Australian "digger". In the assault on Sattelberg (New Guinea) in November 1943, Derrick displayed great leadership and courage, for which

ANECDOTES

he received the Victoria Cross. Just as the attack was looking to have been futile, he took charge and engaged the enemy at close quarters with grenades. He then led his men in destroying ten enemy posts and held the ground during the night. It was fitting that next day that Derrick was the one who raised the Australian flag over Sattelberg. Derrick's exploits brought him to wide public attention; he was a legendary figure in the 9th Division. When he returned to his battalion as a lieutenant from an officer training course, "there was great jubilation".

From "50 Australians" – Australian War Memorial.

Values-Based Leadership

The behaviour of a group that is in pursuit of a goal is generally guided by external rules and the group's internal values. The advantage of values over rules as a guide to group behaviour is the adaptability they provide in ambiguous situations. If an Australian bush fire-fighting unit values 'initiative' above 'procedure', they may well use an appliance in an unconventional manner in order to extinguish a blaze. Within a group or organisation, values-based leadership means that group members will be guided in their decisions and actions by the group's agreed (and hopefully their own) values. Values-based leadership (VBL), therefore, is a general leadership notion for any organisation where the behaviour of leaders reflects their values and sets the example for others in the organisation.

VBL, however, does not automatically mean that leadership outcomes are universally good. VBL as a concept can apply equally to a terrorist organisation or to a hospital. The difference in how outcomes are achieved within these two groups, however, comes down to the values that form the basis of their leadership. Both groups could well share the values of courage, teamwork and initiative. It is unlikely, however, that the terrorist organisation would embrace the values of compassion, freedom, tolerance and the respect and dignity of all persons.

Values-Based Leadership in the Military.

Professional military values tend to be more complementary to 'followership' in battle than they are to leadership in non-operational environments. Professional military values like courage, loyalty and selfless commitment lead to behaviours that are highly desirable in operational situations. Although few in the military would want to see professional military values down-played in the operational context, it is important to remember that these values alone are not a sufficient basis for leadership in all military situations. Militaries require their leaders to carry out their duties well in both peacetime and operational environments. Therefore, military leaders need to also embrace values that underpin both the law of the country and the rules of engagement. Values such as 'care', 'compassion' and 'respect' form the basis for sound leadership in peacetime, even though these values are less applicable to the battlefield situation.

Values-Based Leadership in the ADF

The ADF's "PLICIT" values are also more complementary to 'followership' in battle than they are to leadership in non-operational environments. The PLICIT values of courage, loyalty and teamwork are indeed relevant to a group-based organisation that is involved in intrinsically dangerous undertakings. Nevertheless, these values alone do not make a substantial basis for the activity of leadership that, by its nature, has a focus on relationships and follower aspirations. This issue is addressed by the ADF through: (1) the amplification of the values 'integrity' and 'professionalism'; and (2) the recognition that ADF members also embrace Australian civic values.

The legitimacy of the ADF requires that it embody the same values and beliefs as the Australian society that it defends. The Government's use of the ADF also reflects community values about Australia's ability, where it can, to seek to resist international aggression, relieve human suffering, promote justice and freedom internationally, and protect our borders.

The ADF Leadership Model

The ADF Leadership Model, illustrated below, is a model that indicates the causal chain, where desired leadership behaviours are underpinned by leadership capabilities, performance principles and ADF Values:

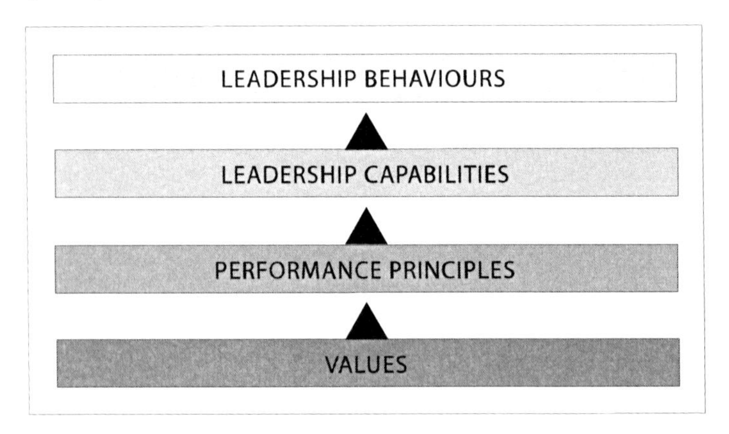

FIGURE 5: The ADF Leadership Model

Performance Principles

The performance principles and leadership capabilities listed below are aligned to the very comprehensive Australian Defence Organisations Leadership Proficiency Framework. Together they form the basis for appropriate leadership behaviour in the ADF.

PERFORMANCE PRINCIPLE	LEADERSHIP CAPABILITY	LEADERSHIP BEHAVIOUR
Challenge People like a challenge and set new performance standards when they are clear about our purpose and understand where their contribution fits in	Set the standard for performance Associates with "Achieves Results" from the Leadership Proficiency Framework	• Articulate and communicate performance expectations • Explain where people's contribution fits in • Exemplify the standard and encourage/assist others to perform to the standard • Measure performance and reward/sanction appropriately
Elbow-room People are responsible, accountable, exercise self-direction and self-control when their supervisor involves them in decisions affecting their workplace and allows them to do their job	Give meaningful direction Associates with "Strategic Thinking" from the Leadership Proficiency Framework	• Involve people in decision-making • Communicate the objective with clarity • Link direction to corporate goals • Ensure people have what they need to get the job done, within resources allocated
Feedback People exercise imagination, and creativity to solve problems when they get constructive feedback on their ideas and are confident that communication lines are open	Make communication a priority Associates with "Communication" from the Leadership Proficiency Framework	• Tell it as it is • Make sure messages are understood • Listen and respond • Actively create a trusting environment
Self-esteem People who feel good about themselves do good work when their supervisor recognises a job well done – praise from supervisors does wonders for self-esteem	Create the climate for success Associates with "Relationships" from the Leadership Proficiency Framework	• Take an interest in people as individuals • Explain people's roles in the organisational direction • Value and acknowledge people's contribution • Recognise people by name
Pride People are proud of the job they do and the organisation they work for when the organisation is making a meaningful contribution to society, engendering trust and mutual respect	Persist until the job's well and truly done Associates with "Personal Drive and Integrity" from the Leadership Proficiency Framework	• Celebrate the team's achievements • Continually review progress and adjust priorities • Help people understand why the job is important • Understand the resources necessary to complete the task

TABLE 1: Performance Principles

Alternative Value Sets

As noted previously, ADF's values and those of the three Service's are roughly congruent and, when combined with other Australian values such as 'trustworthiness' 'care', 'compassion' and 'respect', form a solid basis for leadership. Nevertheless, these values are sometimes "side-lined" by, or even mutated into, alternative value sets. The values espoused by the ADF, such as 'teamwork' and 'integrity', are not necessarily the values that are rewarded within some ADF subcultures. The 'values' of competition, hierarchy and power dominate in some sections of the ADF, as evidenced by the rivalry and blocking tactics between the three Australian services (i.e. competition for resources). The rewarding of alternative values tends to push aside or "sideline" Defence values.

Even more telling is when espoused values are publicly stated but privately punished. Some whistle-blower schemes have failed within subcultures because the person with the moral courage to step forward is branded a "dobber" and ostracised from the work group. In 2003, the media reported a story from a disgruntled member who claimed he was driven from the ADF by his "mates" because the individual alerted the authorities to incidents of marijuana or social drug use within his group.[6]

Essentially, there are always invisible social forces or what can be described as unwritten rules of social order, often with no formal force to back them up, that make it difficult for individuals to act in any way they choose. In fact, any breach of this collective understanding of normal behaviour can draw quite angry reactions. In some groups, this social force is so strong that it is able to mutate Defence values so that they no longer represent their common meaning, but instead take on a meaning particular to that group. In such groups, courage can be seen as stupidity, cowardice can be seen as cunning

[6] *The Weekend Australian Newspaper*, 18 October 2003.

and cruelty can be seen as daring.[7] The torture of cats by a small group of Defence personnel in Queensland is an example where such value mutation has occurred.[8]

Fortunately, conflict between agreed values is more common than their mutation to unsavoury alternatives. Value conflicts arise not so much when there is a choice between good and evil but rather when there is a choice between good and good. Examples include when loyalty to a mate, who has been observed doing wrong, is in conflict with one's own integrity or personal set of rules. Individuals turn a blind eye when a 'good mate' is involved, yet in similar circumstances with other people, they would have taken corrective action. Another less common example of value conflict occurs when an individual's innovative idea is in conflict with the group's concept of teamwork. Bright ideas may never be tested because they are swamped by the power of 'group-think'.

Although there is no real golden rule for knowing 'what ought to be done' in these and other ambiguous situations, two guidelines are supported by the ADF. Firstly, place the Defence value 'integrity' as principle amongst the other Defence values and secondly, before taking action, consider how that action would look next day as a headline in a daily paper or as a lead story in the evening news.

Values Inculcation Through The Affective Domain

Since the affective learning domain provides the key to understanding individual motivation, group dynamics and inter-personal relationships, it is the most important learning domain in leadership development and training. It is through training focused on the affective learning domain that values are inculcated and character is developed. Furthermore, it is how self-discipline eventually replaces imposed discipline.

---

[7] See work done by Dr. Simon Longstaff, 2006.

[8] See *The Age Newspaper*, 12 May 2004; and *The Australian* newspaper 19 November 2004.

External control of behaviour is a time honoured military approach and the basis of military discipline. It is required when members do not understand what is required of them, when members are unwilling to apply the effort required to achieve a task or when members are unwilling to comply with directions, rules or regulations. As a means of exercising influence, however, discipline has some serious limitations. For a start, the exercise of external control is extremely demanding on supervisor time and effort. Secondly, everybody will eventually come across a situation where there is no supervisor and no rule to cover the circumstances. It is in these circumstances that self-discipline, or internally regulated behaviour, becomes a superior mode of operation. Indeed, self-discipline and initiative are key to the ADF endorsed concept of mission command.

Internally regulated behaviour stems from the values held by that individual. A member who values personnel health and fitness will show self-control over food intake and exercise. A member who values conscientiousness will turn to an onerous task even in the absence of supervisor or observation. A person who values honesty will return a found wallet. The advantages in consistency, adaptability and sense of self-worth provided by internal regulation make the inculcation of self-discipline and its associated values a key responsibility of ADF leaders.

Effective leader development comes from having fundamental values that underpin leadership behaviour. Leadership values such as care, compassion, trust, integrity, respect, tolerance and moral courage provide a benchmark against which leaders may reflect on and judge their actions. The following anecdote is an illustration of compassion towards the enemy in time of war.

ANECDOTES

Captain John Collins, RAN, in his cruiser HMAS *Sydney* attacked an Italian destroyer in June 1940. The destroyer rolled over and sank. *Sydney* searched for two hours for survivors and picked up 47 of them during the night. Captain Collins decided that it was no longer prudent to remain searching for the last few who could still be heard somewhere out in the darkness. To give them a fighting chance when it came to dawn, he ordered that one of the ship's sea boats, complete with oars, sails, water and food, be left behind. As a final gesture of compassion he had a searchlight shone on it for a few seconds to draw attention to it as *Sydney* was leaving. As the Italian survivors were landed in Alexandria their surgeon asked that their thanks be conveyed to Captain Collins for the treatment they had received at his hands.

Moral Development in the ADF

The relationship between the development of ethical reasoning, internalised values and self-discipline is strong. The behaviour of young ADF recruits is at first externally controlled by the use of rules and regulations through imposed discipline. Although effective, this method of behaviour control is time consuming and collapses when the rules do not extend to an unexpected situation. Similarly, in the early stages of moral or ethical development, an individual defines right or wrong in terms of what results in rewards or punishment. Overuse of the directive style of leadership simply reinforces moral retardation. It is the ADF leader's responsibility to encourage individuals to break free from the shackles of this early moral development stage and progress to a more "internally controlled" state. When certain values are internalised and used to regulate individual behaviour, the need for regulations and constant supervision diminishes. Not surprisingly, there is a similar progression in the development of ethical or moral reasoning. At higher levels of moral development, an individual stops defining right and wrong in terms of rules and punishment and instead develops internal moral principles that define right and wrong from a universal-values point of view. This is why the inculcation of civil and military values is so important. A simple example of this progression is when someone decides not to bully subordinates because of the value of human dignity rather than any fear of punishment. ADF leaders are responsible for the development of their people through both modelling moral and values-based behaviour and encouraging discussion and reflection on moral or ethical dilemmas.

A Brief Description of the Continuum of ADF Leadership Development

ADF recruit courses are important in initiating leadership training. The primary emphasis of recruit training is given to followership. To this end, group responsibilities are imposed (e.g. area responsibility, group rotational duties, and collective responsibility for group advancement (the award of flashes)). In addition, recruits participate regularly in group activities (e.g. drill and ceremonial, military challenge activities, team sport and the shared experience of adventurous training). The effect of these activities is to expose many recruits to the concept of teamwork, and the development of a Service identity and esprit de corps. Recruits are made progressively aware of the requirements and functioning of the chain-of-command, and of the power of group response and of united action.

The recruit's exposure to leadership concepts is continually maintained through the example of the section leading seaman or corporals, and their model behaviour and maintenance of standards. Introductions to leadership responsibilities are delivered through rotational duties as course orderlies, as section commanders and as executive members of recruit committees. The recruit course provides an effective platform on which to base further leadership development opportunities that will present themselves after graduation.

The Leading Seaman or Corporal rank generally presents the 'first line' of ADF leadership and is the first promotional rank. The duties of leading seaman and corporals involve immediate supervision in a daily, direct, face-to-face and hands-on role. The new leading seaman or corporal is encountering his or her first sustained level of leadership responsibility. Previous exposure is generally limited to Recruit School and workplace models. To enable the leading seaman and corporal to adapt to the new role, the training need is to adopt appropriate leadership attitudes and behaviours. Because of this, functional leadership models are used by the ADF for leading seaman and corporal leadership training. Students are exposed to the concept that leaders are recognised by what they 'say and do'. Leadership checklists are provided, not as a fail-safe recipe to leadership but as a guide and confidence booster. These checklists are accompanied by functional models, such as the John Adair model, to underpin decision-making and the balancing of priorities. Training is generally over a two or three-week period. To maximise this limited time, 'leadership' is linked to virtually every element of the course (e.g. how Service and ADF values are evidenced and demonstrated, by the leading seaman or corporal, in the workplace). Training is conducted in the principles of decision-making, setting and maintenance of standards, delegation, motivation, team discipline and conflict resolution. Training is also conducted in subordinate development and On-Job Training. Adventure Training type exercises are conducted on course where each student will act as section head. Tasks are conducted in the construction of field defences, patrolling, control of a check point, coordination of range cards, and the developments of a key point and its personnel and active and passive drills. Students additionally understudy the position and responsibilities of section leader.

The Petty Officer or Sergeant are normally employed as team leaders. While the involvement continues to be in a daily, face-to-face role, the rank should not be underestimated as ADF work groups vary considerably in size. The role confronting the newly promoted petty officer or sergeant is one of extending the functional level delivered on the leading seaman or corporal course. Training needs to cope with the increasing range of workplace variables for which he, or she, is now responsible. The training models selected for use at this level of training are 'situational'. The new petty officer or sergeant is now required to adapt his previously-learned behaviours to the most appropriate of a range of approaches (i.e. directing, coaching, supporting, delegating). An accurate appraisal of the situation is used to determine the most appropriate and effective alternative. The primary model used Blanchard's 'Situational Leadership II'.

Again, the brief time constraint determines that 'leadership' underpins the conduct of virtually every course outcome. Items of Service culture (e.g. history, customs, rules and traditions) are closely related to petty officer or sergeant workplace attitudes and behaviours. In alignment with the increased scope of their leadership concerns, students also receive training in personnel assessment (PAR), interpersonal and workplace relationships; and the rights, obligations and responsibilities of contractors and public servants in Defence. Training is conducted in the establishment of concurrent activities, daily routines, tactical movement, and sleep and stress management.

The workplace role of the Chief Petty Officer (CPO)/Flight Sergeant/WO2 is to lead more than one team or work group, and to coordinate their activities and outputs. The Chief Petty Officers act as the workplace intermediary of their warrant officer, and are identified as the NCO with the highest levels of personal, workplace interactions. The increased need for personal interaction determines this faculty as the training need for newly promoted CPO/Flight Sergeant/Warrant Officer (WO)2 as a logical continuation of their previous leadership training. The ADF has selected a 'Professional Capability Framework' that encompasses technical expertise, generic skills, diagnostic maps and emotional intelligence (EI). The EI approach isolates the elements responsible for individual success, and identifies them as 'competencies' that are capable of transfer through competency-based training. Again, 'leadership' (and EI) are closely related to other course outcomes to maximise the training's effectiveness. This involves the relationship of EI to project management. Other roles involve the personal interactions required for the management of rosters, and project management supervision.

The workplace role of the ADF Warrant Officer has characteristics that are the most 'managerial', of the NCO ranks. Contact with the workforce is less immediate and face-to-face; and may be primarily maintained through the other Sr NCO ranks. Warrant officers are promoted on the basis of long-term and proven leadership capabilities. Their new role, however, has placed a distance between themselves and their formerly, highly-interactive workplace. Learning to adapt to a less direct leadership role is the primary training need of the newly promoted warrant officer. Students are also introduced to concepts of single service command and control, and the joint method of military appreciation (JMAP). The warrant officer's training needs are related more closely to self-development than their previous training, and—as their leadership is now perceived from a distanced workplace—to the image that they produce. Consequently, Covey's '7 Habits' has been selected as the most appropriate tool; with its emphases on many higher level issues of leadership (e.g. self-management, interdependence, mentoring, stress and time management).

As the continuum of leadership training is continually evolving, one role of the warrant officer course is to gain an overview of their subordinates' leadership development. An awareness of their subordinates' levels of training is important for the new warrant officer to make the best and most informed use of their staff. The remaining content of the warrant officer course links easily with their leadership training. The training includes representing the Defence organisation in the civilian community, and performing the duties of a Discipline Officer.

Officer Leadership Continuum (Cadet to Lieutenant-Colonel or equivalent)

Much like the NCO leadership training continuums, leadership development for ADF officers is carried out by the individual Services. The large exception to this rule is the joint education and training conducted by the Australian Defence College (ADC). About one third of all ADF officers commence their careers at the Australian Defence Force Academy (ADFA), the first and largest of ADC's three joint components. Over a three-year period, ADFA cadet and midshipmen undergo a thorough leadership development program that culminates with a five-day practical exercise that requires each graduate to lead a small team in a military environment. Coverage of leadership theory is also very thorough and the three-year period of training allows for reflection and opportunities to take up leadership positions within the cadet body. Cadets and midshipman study self-esteem, morality of conflict and ethics in leadership amongst many other topics. To align and prepare for their single Service programs, cadets and midshipmen cover both Adair's functional model and Blanchard's 'Situational Leadership II' model of leadership.

The junior officer workplace can vary considerably. The general assumption, however, is of a workplace containing diverse groups (of Service personnel, public servants, and civilian employees and contractors). Junior officers generally work under a level of senior officer supervision, as 'first line' leaders with high levels of interaction with Service subordinates. As leaders at the tactical level, junior officers need a comprehensive understanding of the level of leadership training of each subordinate rank. Their expectations of subordinate performances can be based on this understanding. While their own training needs are at this tactical, 'operator' level, their level of responsibility—and the possibilities offered by the longer course duration—allow this training to be refined to a greater extent. Within the single Service environment non-ADFA officers also cover functional and situational leadership, as well as some elements of EI, as undertaken by the NCO courses.

Training is undertaken to the extent necessary to familiarize the junior officer with subordinate levels of training; and to provide a basis that will enable them to extend their own leadership development, using more complex models. A number of Service specific models have been selected to achieve this end. The RAAF uses the 'Parson's model', the Army uses its concentric circle 'Army Leadership Model' and the Navy uses a version of the 'Defence People Leadership Model'. All of these models attempt to integrate the most desirable elements of a wide cross-section of theories, to their specific military context.

Leadership training is undertaken in a series of escalating increments across the initial officer course. In a series of primarily field exercises and practical work-related applications, junior officers are exposed to scenarios of increasing demand and complexity. To acquaint them intimately with the functions of their subordinates, Navy students undertake a four week initial training cruise while RAAF students undertake a week-long ground defence exercise in which students undertake all of the roles associated with each rank. These activities provide a background of realistic expectation, a basis for empathy, and a foundation for their culminating role as an officer in charge (OIC) of a small team.

Lieutenant-Commander, Major or Squadron Leader

The mid-ranking officer represents the link between the workplace and senior levels of the institution; it is the first level of senior officer rank. The major's role is to act as the intermediary for higher level strategic direction, and to coordinate the functions and outputs of larger work groups, that are generally under the control of junior officers. The major is the senior officer rank with the highest volume of personal, workplace interactions. In a real sense, the major occupies a middle ground between staff and command roles.

As such, a high proportion of Major (equivalents) will undertake the one-year Australian Command and Staff Course (ACSC). The rank has a need to understand the 'bigger picture' concerns of his or her superiors, and interpret them for the direction and development of his or her junior officer subordinates. The ability to function effectively in this dual role is the aim of Single Service PMET training at this rank. Training is given in the structure of higher level Service and ADF command and its doctrines and processes. The short duration of Single Service courses determines that the focus is primarily operational. Leadership models are used to initially focus on 'self', and then extend their concerns to workplace relationships and subordinate development. Myers-Briggs initiates a process of self-knowledge, which is then extended through EI training in self-awareness, self-regulation and motivation.

Emphasis on relationship with subordinates is based on concepts and processes drawn primarily from mission command. A workplace culture is created, in which the subordinates are confident of their empowerment to be self-directive and innovative—when occasion demands—to carry through their commander's intent. Training for the command roles of Major and equivalents includes presentations and experiential case studies in Service doctrine, and in strategic level planning and command in the ADF. Presentations include HQAST and joint operations, and the application of JMAP. Training is also delivered in workforce planning, and the appropriation and financial management systems. A course emphasis is placed, throughout, on effective interpersonal and workplace relations, the management of stress and fatigue, and the reinforcement of ADF values and culture.

Commander, Lieutenant-Colonel, Wing Commander Training and Education

The lieutenant-colonel or equivalent rank in the Navy or Air Force occupies a senior management position, at a level of unit command responsibility. The lieutenant-colonel frequently occupies a position 'at arms length' from the workplace, in which his contact is often maintained through the intermediary of the majors. The newly promoted lieutenant-colonel encounters a new role which obliges them to meet strategic-level Service goals, from a position that places them at an unaccustomed distance from their formerly, highly interactive workplace. The training need is one of adapting to a less direct leadership role. The training needs of a lieutenant-colonel are more closely related to self-development, than any other rank level previously encountered. Their leadership is now perceived from a more distanced workforce, and it requires their high level of sensitivity to the 'image' that they produce. Covey's '7 Habits of Effective Leadership' is once again used, as it appears to offer the most appropriate emphases to higher (boardroom) issues of leadership. The lieutenant-colonel course is developed as a coherent extension of its predecessor, and involves more intensive and higher order involvement with senior Defence management. The course consists of a series of visits and interactions with Defence organisations (including those involved with Human Resource management, financial management, and strategic level operational planning). Exposure to the roles, expectations and responsibilities of commanding officers is also achieved, by selective attendance at the Single Service's Commanding Officer Courses.

Preparing for the Fight After Iraq: The Preparation of One and Two-Star General Officers for Joint Appointments

A major development is underway in regard to developing Australia's most senior military leaders. In June 2006, about 3,000 ADF personnel were deployed in four discrete theatres of operations. Experience since 1999 in East Timor suggested that the ADF needed to place more emphasis on the development of the commanders who would lead Australia's next operation, wherever that may be. One senior ADF officer stated in 2006:

> *Our commanders are ill-prepared to conduct modern warfighting. Lack of experience is understandable, but lack of training and education is unforgivable. Our joint commander education is at best mediocre, and has missed certain constants and certain changes in the nature of modern warfare. In particular, the uncompromising nature of modern warfare is not reflected in our Professional Military Education system.*

In preparing this new course, the ADF also considered Professor Eliot Cohen's observation that "the historical mind, however, knows that the most important determinants of outcomes in war are often the strengths and weaknesses of individual commanders and their decisions." As such, the Defence Portfolio Evaluation Report (PER) titled 'The Preparation of ADF Officers for Joint Appointments' from November 2005 made the following recommendation, that:

> *A short 'top-up' programme be developed for one and two star officers to prepare them for short notice command and key staff appointment roles in Australia or overseas, and for roles as component commanders. The programme should cover the latest relevant joint and combined doctrine, relevant government policy and decision-making on pertinent national security issues, and the conduct of inter-agency and multi-national operations in the context of Australia's strategic goals and directives. The programme should also cover key national policies and objectives, as well as up to the minute international perspectives and implications, and other topical issues that are likely to impinge on their future appointment.*

The purpose would be to prepare a pool of selected officers for specific roles in higher-level headquarters and for command and key staff appointments in short notice joint and coalition operations.

The aim of the new course, planned to be underway in late 2006, will be to prepare selected one and two-star general officers for command and key staff appointments in joint and coalition operations in Australia or overseas. It is accepted that the course would need to be reviewed at least every two years to remain abreast of international security developments. The nature of the course suggests that it would be a mix of command and leadership training and education. Some elements would clearly be focused on developing a specific skill set for the future command and staff role whilst others would be focused on how to think about the challenges of the role.

The basis of the course andragogical philosophy will be a process of mental inquiry incorporating elements of the Socratic dialogue where the leader or course member poses a question or dilemma and the course members pool their thinking and experience to seek an answer or solution. Scholars have noted, "Adult education is a process through which learners become aware of significant experience. Recognition of significance leads to evaluation. Meanings accompany experience when we know what is happening and what importance the event includes for our personalities." Lindeman further summarised a series of key assumptions about adult learners:

- Adults are motivated to learn as they experience needs and interests that learning will satisfy.
- Adults' orientation to learning is life-centred.
- Experience is the richest source for adults' learning.
- Adults have a deep need to be self-directing.
- Individual differences among people increase with age.

Scholar David Kolb is a leader in emphasising the practice of experiential learning and he has produced a model with suggested learning strategies:

Kolb's Stage	Example Learning /Teaching Strategy
Concrete experience	Simulation, Case Study, Real Experience, Field trip, Demonstrations
Observe and Reflect	Discussion, Small Groups, Designated Observers
Abstract Conceptualisation	Sharing content
Active Experimentation	OJT experience, Practice sessions (wargaming)

TABLE 2: Kolb's Stage

In addition, Professor Wlodowski believes that adult motivation to learn is the sum of the four factors of success, volition, value and enjoyment. These learning principles have been incorporated in developing what will be a practical, hands-on course.

In the United States (US), several organisations utilise 'learning contracts' to pursue professional educational goals at the executive level. The one and two-star general officer rank students develop a written agreement with their senior mentor which outlines their educational goals over say the next two years. It seems to work with the US Navy and will be considered in the development of this course.

The nature of the course suggests a need for a facilitator in some sessions and selected 'greybeards' to act in mentoring roles. Care will need to be taken in this regard. Experience with the US Navy executive leadership programme at the Naval Post Graduate School at Monterey indicates that just because you have been a three or four-star general does not mean that you are necessarily suitable as a mentor. On the other hand, the Luck/Franks relationship appeared to have worked very well in Iraq. The selected mentors will be engaged beyond the tenure of the course. In the ADF context, mentors may include selected former Service chiefs and other senior commanders. The critical point is that the ADF uses mentors who have 'done things' in its recent corporate experience.

Command: The Australian Way

In 2000, the ADF produced a study, as a result of a direction by the Chief of the Defence Force, into the style of Australian Command. The Centre assumed responsibility for the further development of this work in 2002, and it remains the foundation for all command research that is currently underway at the ADC. The study, by retired Brigadier Maurie Meecham, reported that the approach to warfighting, and particularly to command by most militaries, is influenced by a range of cultural, national and global factors. While there are many similarities in approaches to command, each nation has a unique set of factors that give it a distinct philosophy of command.

Even in the short history of the ADF, significant evolution has occurred in the area of command. Initially, Britain provided forces and commanders for the Australian colonies, and even after Federation, with a few exceptions, Australia relied heavily on Britain for senior commanders and guidance on defence matters. After World War II, the influence of the United States increased and reached a peak during the war in Vietnam. However, since the end of that war, and particularly during the 1980s and 1990s, the ADF has taken a more independent stance and continued to develop an approach which better meets its own unique cultural and geo-strategic factors.

The study concluded that the distinctly Australian philosophy of command is characterised by effective people – focused leadership, trust and confidence between all ranks and a sound understanding of the intentions of one's superior. It is also characterised by the taking of calculated risks and a reliability of responses at every level based primarily on a sound system of doctrine.

These fundamental ideas on command apply equally to Naval, Army, Air Force and Joint activities in peace and in conflict. While the Australian approach has much in common with the command philosophies of our closest friends and allies, it has a distinctly Australian character. It is a way of thinking and behaving which is flexible and versatile, and it suits the Australian character. Although successful ADF commanders have exercised their authority in much the same way for decades, the environment in which today's and future commanders will operate has changed.

Conclusion

In 2004, American General Tommy Frank stated:

> *All the way down to the tactical level I found the same situation. The 'flash to bang' time for planning by the Australians for the conduct of tactical or operational – level missions was always very quick and efficient. The commitments made were always solid and the Australians showed up when and where they said they would, whether we were talking about naval power, air power or special operations. They never disappointed me . . . Australia had a very competent military force. There was never any confusion; there was never any bullshit.'*
>
> General Tommy Franks, 2004.

The ADF continues to place great emphasis on the development of its leaders to support and implement its vision of being "balanced, networked, deployable, staffed by dedicated and professional people, excelling at joint, interagency and coalition operations." It places great emphasis on preparing leaders at all levels of the organisation and is cognisant of the expectations of the "X" and "Y" generations. The extensive leadership development programmes are also tempered by the wide range of recent operational experience. And ADF leaders continue to prove themselves on operations, whether it be hunting Taliban in Afghanistan, saving lives in tsunami affected Sumatra, or disarming rival factions in East Timor.

The Leadership Proficiency Framework will be introduced later in 2006. It will identify the generic capabilities and behaviours (the 'core' proficiencies) required by all employees in Defence. Over the next few years the 90,000 employees in Defence will share a common leadership language.

With regard to preparing ADF leaders for the complex ethical environment in which they are operating now and in the future, more time needs to be set aside to debate the big issues at the ADF's professional military education institutions. For the foreseeable future the military ethics program development responsibility will remain at the Centre for Defence Leadership Studies. The issues continue to emerge and at the time of writing, the cases of Lieutenant-Commander Robyn Fahey (a discrimination and harassment incident that has been dragging on in the Navy for six years) and Private Jake Kovco (shot in a non-combat related incident in Iraq in April 2006) are very much in the public and media spotlight. The ADF also awaits the findings of the Board of Inquiry into the Navy Sea King crash that killed nine personnel in Indonesia in April 2005.

Australia's recent operational experience shows that modern technology and tough, well-trained people can create a warfighting advantage. It is this combination of people and technology that makes the concept of Network Centric Warfare (NCW) so important to the future of the ADF. The Australian definition of NCW is "a means of organising the force by using modern information technology to link sensors, decision-makers and weapons systems to help people work more effectively to achieve the commander's intent." This definition highlights that NCW is more than a concept or collection of new technologies, but rather is a tool that can contribute significantly to producing a warfighting advantage. The human dimension of NCW recognises that the network includes people; people who make decisions, crew platforms, fight and lead. This dimension highlights the importance of high standards of training and education; the ability to cope with volatility, uncertainty, complexity and ambiguity; and the ability to make judgements that have lethal consequences; all the time ensuring that the ADF maintains its legitimacy as a fighting force. People provide strength to the network by applying their leadership, skills, and experience in transforming data into action. They are the 'glue' that binds the network. But people must be trained and educated to deal with the increased demands that this networked environment will place upon their skills, competencies and physical and mental abilities. This is where leadership will give the ADF the capability edge. There is little doubt that events in the so-called 'arc of instability' to Australia's north will continue to test the command and leadership skills of the ADF into the second decade of the 21st century.

CHAPTER 2

Emerging from a Decade of Darkness:

The Creation of the Canadian Forces Leadership Institute

Colonel Bernd Horn and Lieutenant-Colonel Allister MacIntyre

Unfortunately, dramatic change is normally the result of significant failure. Very rarely can large institutions bring themselves to drastically change organizational culture or practices unless there is an overwhelming catalyst. This was no different for the Department of National Defence (DND) and the Canadian Forces (CF) during the 1990s, when they, particularly the officer corps, found themselves in a difficult and deteriorating situation. A series of scandals over questionable behaviour by DND and CF members both at home and abroad triggered a frenzy of media attention. Opulent spending practices by senior officers, as well as incidents of drunkenness and black marketeering overseas were just some examples of the objectionable behaviour. However, the torture killing of a Somali detainee by Canadian soldiers in March of 1993, and the subsequent mishandling of the affair by DND, brought the systemic problems to a head. By 1997, the CF had imploded and military leaders found themselves at the lowest ebb of their history. They had lost the confidence and trust of the government and Canadian people they served. They were stripped of their ability to investigate themselves. Furthermore, they were not trusted to implement the recommended changes forced upon them by the government and an external committee was established as a watchdog to change. Whether the leadership wanted to admit it or not, and they vehemently tried to deny it at the time, there existed some substantial and deep rooted problems with DND, the CF and the Canadian officer corps. They were caught in a decade of darkness.

The road to this sad state was a long one. The assault on the CF and its senior leadership in the late 1980s and into the 1990s was cataclysmic. The safe, templated and well-known Cold War paradigm disappeared almost overnight. The new security environment marked by confusion, ambiguity, ever present media, and nefarious enemies and threats embedded in the context of failed and failing states overloaded a traditional, conservative and intellectually inflexible officer corps that saw the world in terms of absolutes. As if this was not enough, a government perched on a veritable crumbling fiscal precipice looked to the military and a perceived "peace dividend" to solve part of its problem.

These pressures, not surprisingly stressed the CF. Scandals, and the bungled attempts at dealing with them, led to the loss of government trust. This was monumental. Equally so, however, was the effect on Canadian society. As the military's failures, notably incidents of wrongdoing overseas, as well as reports of opulent and / or unethical spending and behaviour by senior leaders surfaced, Canadians quickly became incensed. Exacerbating this situation was a DND leadership that was not accustomed to criticism or scrutiny by the public. The clear and present Soviet threat and spectre of nuclear Armageddon had always been enough to distract and silence critics. So they did what they had always done – ignore the noise long enough and it will go away. They refused to explain themselves or provide information. They ignored or stonewalled queries, believing that the storm would simply blow over. If the winds were too strong, they could always shelter behind the well-tested barrier of "national security" and the condescending, if not arrogant, attitude that civilians should just leave military business to the professionals.

However, catastrophically, similar to their inability to anticipate, adapt or change to the transformation in the security environment, sphere of military affairs and operations, the CF completely missed the dramatic and profound societal shift. As a result, they lost the confidence and trust of the very people for which they existed to serve – Canadian society. The CF had dropped into the abyss. They had lost the confidence of both the government and people of Canada.

So, what happened? Much like most militaries, the Canadian armed forces throughout its history has been a very conservative and anti-intellectual institution. Moreover, Canada, much like most western nations, did not believe in large standing armies. However, in the aftermath of the Second World War, when two distrustful and ideologically opposed superpowers emerged from that conflict, the world changed dramatically. Exacerbating the political and military competition between the former allies of convenience was technology. The war had sparked exponential advancements in warfare; jet engines, advanced aircraft carriers and submarines, rockets and atomic and nuclear weapons made the world that much smaller, and countries that much more vulnerable.

By 1949, the West had created the North Atlantic Treaty Organization (NATO) as a hedge against perceived Soviet intentions at westward expansion. Soon after, the Soviets created the Warsaw Pact, dragooning its occupied territories into an alliance to protect them from their fear of Western aggression. And so, Europe became divided by an "iron curtain" and soon fell into a military stand-off, if not an arms race. This European centric contest soon leaked into a global contest – with much of the world falling into one camp or another. Faced with the prospect of nuclear Armageddon if the major antagonists faced off directly, the superpower competition soon played itself out in proxy wars in Korea, Africa, and the Middle East.

Throughout one thing was always certain, or at least one was led to believe it was – the Cold War was just a breath away from becoming a hot war, one laden with consequence should the superpowers turn to their nuclear arsenals. And so, from 1949, the world was seemingly on the brink of disaster. Securing the Western way of life for a grateful citizenry were large standing armies prepared to do battle with the Soviet hordes. This state of affairs had a great impact on Canada and its armed forces. For the first time in its history, it maintained a large standing army. In fact, it deployed a large force overseas – including a heavy mechanized brigade group and a wing of fighter aircraft. This NATO commitment quickly became the raison d'être of the CF and all but consumed its entire focus.

The Cold War despite its possible consequences, however, was in retrospect a simple era for the military – if not its hey day. The threat seemed frighteningly real. Pictures of huge missiles pointed towards North America, impressive May Day parades in Moscow that revealed a large and very lethal military arsenal, the continued occupation of territory liberated from Germany in World War II and the brutal suppression of nationalist movements therein, reinforced the need for large Western forces. And in the event this was not enough, every year (coincidently around budget appropriation time) the US Department of Defense published its glossy *The Soviet Menace*, which showcased the Soviet Union's bulging military arsenal. In sum, governments and the public at large could easily recognize the threat. Accordingly, the military was provided with the necessary budget and left alone to secure the Western way of life in the prosperous, booming post-war era.

For the military, this was significant. They had a clear mission – counter the Soviet threat. And its implementation was left largely to the professionals. National security dictated secrecy and the Soviet's active espionage campaigns, which often were made quite public once compromised, reinforced the need for a heavy cloak of secrecy on all things military. As a result, the military could easily, and it did, hide behind this veil to avoid explaining those things it would rather not discuss. Not surprisingly, at times this list was quite large. However, the threat mitigated disclosure and the public was content not to interfere, trusting its politicians and military professionals were acting in the best interest of the state. Therefore, a very closed mindset, one that avoided public disclosure, if not almost totally contemptuous of it, developed. Quite simply, the military knew best – and those who did not serve could not possibly understand the context of national security. Therefore, the military was largely allowed to work on its own (within the context of its national institution and NATO framework) with little interaction with the outside world.

A second aspect of the simplicity of the Cold War was the operating security environment. The world was largely divided into two spheres (i.e. NATO / Warsaw Pact) and each was careful not to interfere dramatically in the other's. The actions and non-actions of such events as the Hungarian Revolution in 1956, the Cuban Missile Crisis in 1962, and the Czechoslovakian Revolution in 1967 provide clear examples of the unwritten understanding that existed. Supporting insurgents or proxy wars in theatres around the world (e.g. Vietnam, Middle East, Angola, Afghanistan) were always carefully managed. Rarely would the superpowers allow themselves to come into direct confrontation. Both camps understood and largely abided by the unwritten rules. Equally important, both camps propped up their surrogate, proxy and / or supported allies, and ensured they maintained the global status quo. All together, this provided a great deal of stability during the Cold War.

Even peacekeeping during this period fell into the clearly understood model. Peacekeepers were only employed when both antagonists agreed to their presence. Their role was to monitor a ceasefire or peace agreement once the fighting had stopped. Their employment, therefore, was always within a prescribed boundary – in the buffer zone between the two former warring parties. Their operating environment was very clear. Each side had its fortified line. Each side was clearly delineated by its front line and all participants were in clearly identifiable national uniforms. Moreover, the entire operational area was quarantined. There were rarely civilians or press to deal with. When there were, it was under carefully controlled and escorted circumstances. Once again, the military was allowed to operate in almost complete isolation. The relative simplicity of the operating security environment bled into the very fabric of the institution. The Cold War bred a very techno-centric culture. What became important was one's capability as a proficient technical warfighter. After all, the enemy was almost perfectly symmetrical – almost a carbon copy of its antagonist. Inventories and tactics were designed to fight a conventional (and possibly nuclear) war against forces of a similar type. Everything was templated. Soldiers, non-commissioned officers (NCOs) and officers were taught Soviet order of battle and tactics. Exercises revolved around set initiators (e.g. the arrival of the combat reconnaissance patrol of a mechanized motor rifle division), which would indicate exactly what the enemy consisted of and where he was located. Based on the distances from friendly front lines, it could now be determined what tactics he would adopt

In essence, the key to training was learning the enemy's order of battle. As such, training institutions provided lessons, handbooks and exams on the Soviet enemy. Students would memorize the organizational composition (including numbers of personnel, specific weapons and their ranges, vehicles and tactics) from section level to motor rifle division and higher, depending on their respective rank level.

Furthermore, staff tables, NATO reports and returns and common doctrinal publications simplified operating procedures and tactics. NATO policy, dictated largely by the "Big Boys" of the organization, relieved Canada of much of the burden of strategic, as well as operational, decision making. Canada's tactical role, whether on the Central Front in Germany or its Allied Command Europe (ACE) AMF(L) [ACE Mobile Force (land)] role in Northern Norway, reinforced the simplicity of the Cold War for the CF. It knew its role, its routes to the front, its actual fighting positions and the exact enemy it would face. As such, much of the training revolved around rehearsals for the possible show down between NATO and the Warsaw Pact on the actual ground and exact fighting positions where this would happen.

Not surprisingly, this templated Cold War paradigm shaped how the CF evolved. Technical expertise and actual experience (particularly in Europe) within the conventional NATO warfighting framework became the key drivers for success. It nurtured a system that relied on the traditional military concept that leadership is a top-down hierarchical action that depends on unit command and staff appointments, specifically experience, as the mechanism to prepare individuals for higher command at the strategic level. Within this model, higher education was not deemed important. It stressed training (a predictable response to a predictable situation) to the virtual exclusion of education (a reasoned response to an unpredictable situation – i.e. critical thinking in the face of the unknown).

In fact, a rabid anti-intellectualism actually thrived. Those seeking higher education (i.e. a Masters Degree – as a PhD was simply unfathomable) were deemed suspect; individuals obviously trying to prepare themselves for a life outside the military. What was important within the military hierarchy were individuals who understood the system – the operating environment; the Soviet enemy; NATO doctrine and SOPs; and Canadian equipment, tactics, and staff work. Significantly, this fervent anti-intellectualism denuded the officer corps of individuals capable of, or willing to undertake, analysis, critical thinking, reflection and visioning in the larger geo-political and societal context. The inherent conservative and traditional military mind frame, compounded by its hierarchical, authoritative and closed structure fed a system that not only ignored, but actively closed itself to, outside thought and criticism.

In the end, the Cold War created a techno-centric, experience-based officer corps that was largely isolated from outside thought or criticism. Its intellectual development was severely limited and depended on simple experience and training, which focused on the application of NATO warfighting doctrine to prepare itself for World War III on the North European plain and adjunct theatres. Not surprisingly, its leadership doctrine was similarly dated, as it revolved around a very industrial era model, which was output related. In essence, if the mission was successful or the task was attained – ergo, the commander showed leadership (whether the task was completed in spite of the commander or not). If the task failed, the commander was obviously let down by his subordinates. Clearly, within such a model, mission success at any cost, became the key factor.

Throughout the Cold War, the system prospered for the most part. Commanders cloned themselves, and thereby ensured the well-being of the institution. Through the years, this myopic view and isolation created an officer corps that was intolerant of criticism, self-scrutiny or wider intellectual stimulation. Experienced Cold War technicians, who did not rock the boat and supported the status quo tended to do well.

By 1987, the newly elected Conservative government and their bold new Defence White Paper, *Challenge and Commitment, A Defence Policy for Canada* was welcomed with open arms. It represented a reinforcement of the Cold War mentality – large conventional forces such as heavy mechanized forces in Germany and nuclear submarines. It also represented a halt to the continual downward spiral of defence spending that started in 1964, with the Liberal White Paper, and remained unabated ever since. However, the Conservative White Paper, much like their government, was fleeting. And, it did not bode well for the CF.

Military commanders and the CF in general continued on their course oblivious to the environment around them. And then, their world collapsed. The Fall of the Berlin Wall in December 1989, which is now universally accepted as the end of the Cold War, left the CF and its leaders at a loss. What now? The Cold War was over. We had won. Moreover, with the war over, everyone expected a peace dividend. And why not? With the Soviet threat eliminated – why maintain large military forces? Moreover, the Canadian government was facing a colossal deficit that was dragging down the national economy, devaluing the Canadian dollar and scaring off foreign investment. So where to find extra money?

Not surprisingly, DND became a natural target. With the largest discretionary budget in the government it was a no-brainer, particularly since the war was over. However, for the CF officer corps it was the beginning of the end. The new world order quickly began to unravel. Former proxies and surrogates, now left to their own devices without the necessary economic subsidies to survive, or the security infrastructure to hold together fragmented ethic and culturally diverse populations, quickly spiralled into chaos. Failed and failing states mushroomed. In their wake, civil war, ethnic cleansing and genocide erupted on the global scene.

Appalled by the scenes of horror and inhumanity beamed into living rooms by the nightly news, publics soon pressured governments to act. As a result, the West, as individual countries, as well as a collective entity under UN auspices, soon dispatched military forces to bring order to the chaos. But, the attempts were awkward and ineffective. The world had changed but not everyone had taken notice. The new missions that politicians and military commanders sent their troops on were not of the Cold War model. Contrived manpower ceilings and equipment tables based on cost control and the desire not to present too warlike an image fell short of providing the troops and the resources they needed on the ground. Attempting humanitarian aid and / or peacekeeping operations in an environment where there was still an active war in progress and where none of the belligerents welcomed the interference of UN troops created frustration, risk, and inefficiencies on the ground for the soldiers. It also showcased the UN's ineffectiveness in the new world order. Unable to reach consensus, unwilling to provide mandates with the necessary level of force and unable to provide the necessary command and control structure to react in a timely and effective manner, missions floundered.

From the CF perspective, troops were sent into harm's way without adequate resources, rules of engagement or coherent engagement policy. At the same time, the CF was deploying a record number of troops on an unprecedented number of operations, its budget was being substantially slashed. From 1989-2001 the CF deployed on approximately 67 missions, compared to 25 missions, during the period 1948-1989. Concurrently, the military budget was slashed 23 percent between 1994-1999 alone.

Exacerbating the crisis in operational tempo and the stress this was placing on CF personnel, a series of incidents began to rock DND. Operations in the Former Yugoslavia, Cambodia, Haiti, Somalia and Rwanda had incidents of unprofessional, and in some cases criminal, behaviour. Questionable shootings, disciplinary infractions (particularly drunkenness), as well as black marketeering and the misappropriation of funds and resources created scandals. Concomitant with the troubles overseas were increasing revelations in Canada of questionable practices, particularly the use of government resources for personal purposes by senior officers in DND. Not surprisingly, the bombardment of negative press eroded the CF's credibility.

Notwithstanding the problems, it was the torture killing of a teenage detainee by Canadian soldiers in Somalia on 16 March 1993 that proved to be the catalyst that sparked the implosion of the CF officer corps. The killing was horrific enough. It tarnished the international image of the "do-gooder" Canadian peacekeeper. Moreover, it assailed the Canadian public's perception of its soldiers who seemingly no longer represented Canadian ideals or values. What made a bad situation worse, however, was DND's response to the crisis. Faced with increasing criticism from the media and the public at large, the senior DND leadership, both civilian and military, decided to stonewall its detractors. Falling back on their Cold War experience and mindset, they attempted to simply ignore the criticism and then, when this failed, they selectively released information, often in a misleading manner. This quickly led to charges of a cover-up at the highest levels in National Defence Headquarters, which later were borne out to be accurate.

The Canadian officer corps had reached a low point in its history. It was unable to foresee, adapt or even realize that the world no longer fit its archaic Cold War paradigm despite the substantial and significant geo-political and societal changes that occurred around them. It was unwilling, or perhaps unable, to realize this. Moreover, as is incumbent on all professions, it was also unwilling, or unable, to maintain its professionalism (i.e., responsibility – special duty to Canada; expertise, identity and vocational ethic). This last failing, specifically its inability to maintain a healthy military ethos (i.e., the values, beliefs and expectations that reflect core Canadian values and the imperatives of military professionalism) was catastrophic. Due to their failing, the Government and people of Canada no longer trusted them to regulate themselves.

An election in 1993 swept in a new Liberal government. Tiring of the public criticism and frustrated with the seeming lack of cooperation from DND, the government stripped the military of its ability to investigate itself and established the *Commission of Inquiry into the Deployment of Canadian Forces to Somalia* to examine the events and causes of the killing in Somalia. Not fully understood by many in the military, this action was seminal. It indicated that the government no longer trusted its military to investigate itself. As such, it stripped a key attribute of any profession from DND – self-regulation. Although many tried to deny the implication, the CF officer corps had reached a new low.

In turn, the Commission, frustrated by an apparently obdurate, if not at times dishonest, officer corps produced a scathing report. Of the 160 recommendations contained in the Somalia Commission Report, 112 were leadership and management related. In sum, the Somalia Commissioners found that "a failure of military values lies at the heart of the

Somalia experience." Of the 160 recommendations contained in the Somalia Commission Report, the Minister of National Defence (MND) accepted 132 for implementation. All told, he endorsed some 250 recommendations for change. These originated from his own Report to the Prime Minister, the Somalia Commission, and recommendations from the *Report of the Special Advisory Group on Military Justice and Military Police Investigative Services*; the *Report on the Quasi-Judicial Role of the Minister of National Defence*; and the *Report of the Special Commission on the Restructuring of the Reserves*. The accepted recommendations covered virtually all aspects of the functioning of DND.

However, the distrust of the military had sunk to such a low level that the government also established a "Minister's Monitoring Committee on Change in the Department of National Defence and the Canadian Forces" (MMC) to "monitor progress with respect to the implementation of change...." General Maurice Baril, a former Chief of the Defence Staff (CDS) conceded, "Undeniably, the 1990s represented the first strong test of the contemporary Canadian officer corps and we found part of it was broken." He added, "experience in and of itself was not enough."

This realization should not have been a revelation. Thirty years earlier, another former CDS had already alluded to the danger. "It matters little whether the Forces have their present manpower strength and financial budget, or half of them, or double them," warned General Jean V. Allard, "without a properly educated, effectively trained, professional officer corps the Forces would in the future be doomed to, at the best mediocrity; at the worst, disaster." His warning went unheeded. But then, so did many others.

However, the crises in the 1990s, combined with the Canadian societal shift, which author Peter C. Newman described as a movement from deference to authority to one of defiance, forced the government and military to transform. No longer could either hide behind a veil of national security.

The public demanded accountability, responsibility and transparency from its government and military. As a result, the message, which had been resisted for so long finally sunk in. "The Army was forced to change," conceded Lieutenant-General Mike Jeffrey, a former commander of the army, "I mean forced." He added, "The challenge is not to forget those institutional failures took place. We had significant failures." This message has not been lost. The tragedy in Somalia sparked a virtual reformation of the CF officer corps and the institution itself. As a result, the 250 recommendations, watched over by the MMC, have been largely instituted. Fundamental to the transformation were the CF Ethics guidelines articulated in 1997, which outlined three key principles: respect the dignity of all persons; serve nation before self; and obey and support lawful authority. This statement was incorporated into all recruiting, training and professional development.

In addition, new appraisal systems and succession planning processes were undertaken, which importantly diluted the influence and power of unofficial "Regimental councils." Moreover, DND established a *Canadian Military Journal* to provide a forum for professional discourse, discussion, and debate, and it undertook a public affairs policy that was based on transparency and accuracy. It also put increasing emphasis on its obligations under the access to information legislation and also introduced a multitude of change initiatives that addressed issues from employment equity, soldier and family quality of life, to more fiscally responsible management practices.

Additionally, due to its strategic failure, DND also put greater emphasis on adaptation, change and proactive vision. As such, it promulgated a number of strategic vision documents such as *Shaping the Future of Canadian Defence: A Strategy for 2020*, in June 1999; *Canadian Officership in the 21st Century* and *People in Defence Beyond 2000*, both in May 2001.

But arguably, one of the critical reforms, which was vehemently resisted initially but that has since taken root, was the recognition and support for an intellectually sound officer corps. After all, "a lack of intellectual discipline in the past," acknowledged former Army Commander Lieutenant-General Mike Jeffrey, "has got us where we are today." As such, the MND directed that beginning in 1997, a university degree was a prerequisite to commissioning as an officer. Moreover, professional development (PD) was extended to include senior officers, including generals. Moreover, formal military PD and staff college courses evolved to include a greater academic content, particularly an emphasis on the humanities / social studies. University study, especially at the graduate level, was not only accepted but actually encouraged; and rightfully so. The many tenets of scholarship, namely precision, detailed research, communications, breadth of knowledge, placing events in a proper economic political and social context, drawing conclusion and trying to discern themes there from, committing those to paper and articulating them so that others can understand the argument put forward and learn from it, are all skills that are necessary for an officer.

Moreover, a greater breadth of knowledge, a tolerance to alternate interpretations and ideas, a comfort with critical debate and discussion, the honing of analytical skills, as well as the exposure to completely new bodies of literature and thought that expand the mind and make the officer that much more capable and professional (i.e., it is an important component of "expertise," which cannot reside exclusively with technical war fighting skills and acumen) <u>was also emphasized</u>. "Officers need to have the right mindset to change and evolve the profession," argued one former CDS, "knowledge must be valued as a key ingredient to our growth as individuals and as a profession."

Importantly, a Canadian Defence Academy (CDA) was established to coordinate all PD for the officer and senior NCO corps. Its organization included a Canadian Forces Leadership Institute (CFLI) that is responsible for research, and the creation and promulgation of doctrine and concept development in regards to leadership and the profession of arms. In short, it is the national centre of excellence for military leadership. It was in fact, CFLI that produced *Duty with Honour: The Profession of Arms in Canada*, a seminal document that captures the theoretical and philosophical underpinnings of the profession of arms and clearly articulates what it means to be a Canadian, or for that matter, any military professional.

In addition, CFLI created and promulgated a new leadership doctrine manual; an undertaking that was decades overdue. A companion volume that articulates the conceptual and theoretical foundation that has guided the development of the CF leadership model and approach accompanied this doctrinal publication. Moreover, applied manuals, focusing on leading people and leading at the institutional level were also produced.

Mission and Vision

When the original concept for CFLI as an institution was developed, the mandate focused solely on leadership research and development. In a letter dated 2 September 1998, Lieutenant-General Romeo Dallaire (then the Commander of the Canadian Forces Recruiting Education and Training System) observed that others had described the leadership in the CF as lacking. He argued that it "is crucial that the initiative is regained, and the avenue for this would be to engage in greater research, development, and academic investigation of leadership." It was his vision that a centre of excellence for leadership would "set the national standard." This initiative eventually led to a February 2001 approval of the CFLI Charter with an establishment of 13 positions (6 Military and 7 Civilian). The preliminary structure contained three leadership cells (theory, applied, and lessons learned) each with three positions, a director holding the rank of Colonel, and three administration positions. The administrative support was heavier than might have been expected because there was a possibility that CFLI would be a relatively self-sustained lodger unit. Although possible arrangements for command and control had been discussed, they were not finalized at that time.

During the summer of 2002, CDA Headquarters was established. Concurrent with the launching of CDA HQ, there was a decision that CFLI, as the champion for leadership throughout the Canadian Forces, would become part of this academy. With the resolution of reporting relationships, the structure of CFLI was amended to eleven positions by reducing the administrative requirement to one position on the assumption that major administrative activities would be centralized for all CDA HQ staff. As will become apparent in the following section, the reality of operating an institution as complex as CFLI has driven the need to augment the administrative side of the house, and the administrative support now stands at two positions.

The mission of CFLI is to generate research, concept development and doctrine in regards to military leadership and the profession of arms to support the generation of effective military leaders. The institute's vision is to be a national centre of excellence for leadership and professionalism research, concept development and doctrine. These ideals were established with the full understanding that recognition of the institute, as a "centre of excellence," was a right that had to be earned. With this notion in mind, CFLI currently studies, and publishes, concepts such as professions and professionalism, leadership theories and models, ethics, and officer and enlisted member roles and relationships. The institute has also actively developed an extensive network with similarly oriented agencies on both a national and international level.

Responsibilities

CFLI has been established to:

1. Develop and disseminate core concepts of leadership and the Profession of Arms to the CF;

2. Encourage scholars and military professionals, both within and outside the military, to share their expertise by contributing chapters and academic papers to the diverse CFLI writing projects thereby ensuring currency and academic credibility;

3. Stimulate and promote an intellectual base for best practices identification, professional development, articulation of core leadership and professional concepts, providing a focus and unity of thought in these domains;

4. Conduct leadership lessons learned, identify emerging concepts and update the professional body of knowledge through preparation of the capstone CF Leadership and Profession of Arms Manuals;

5. Serve as a conduit to academic centres and other government agencies;

6. Strengthen the foundations of CF leadership and professionalism, capitalizing on the wealth of experience in the CF Officers and NCMs; and,

7. Articulate enduring military leadership principles by conducting research, review, analysis, development, synthesis and evaluation of leadership and professionalism.

The organizational structure of CFLI has evolved since the institute was originally established. As can be observed from Figure 1 below, a military Colonel presently commands the institute. Staff members have been drawn from a variety of academic and military backgrounds. For example, the current Director has a PhD in History and War Studies, while his predecessor held a doctorate in psychology. This eclectic configuration was deliberately put in place to ensure that the topics of primary interest (e.g., leadership, professionalism, ethics) would be tackled from as many different perspectives

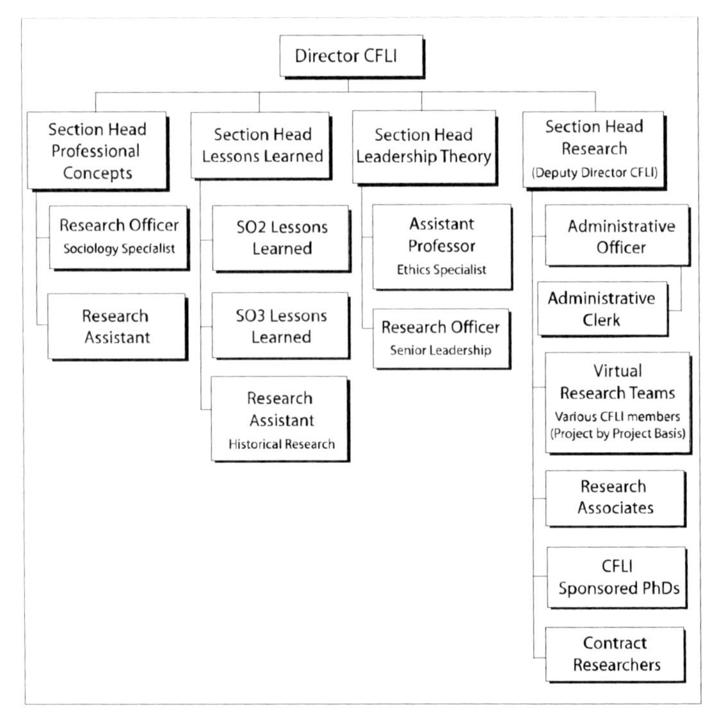

FIGURE 1: Canadian Forces Leadership Institute Organization Chart

as possible. The academic disciplines presently represented within the institute include history, sociology, psychology, political science, international affairs, philosophy, ethics, the military profession, environmental science, research and methodology. Experience has taught us that many of the disciplines are complementary and the result has been a synergistic and enriching work atmosphere.

CFLI is a component of CDA, and CDA is responsible for all common training and education within the Canadian Forces. Consequently, one might expect that CFLI would engage directly in leadership education and training. But, this is not the case. Although members from CFLI have been, on a fairly regular basis, called upon to provide lectures across

Canada and to feed into the developmental and educational process, the actual delivery of training is not part of CFLI's mandate.

Defining Leadership

As mentioned previously, CFLI produced the doctrinal manual *Duty With Honour: The Profession of Arms in Canada* in 2003. This document represents the first time, in Canada, that a clear articulation of what it means to be a member of the profession of arms was developed and presented in such a fashion. As the title suggests, at the heart of the military profession is the notion that there is an expectation that members in uniform will conduct themselves honourably while carrying out their responsibilities. Also as mentioned earlier, two companion doctrinal volumes were published in 2005 that delineate the leadership expectations for the Canadian Forces. The first of these publications, *Leadership in the Canadian Forces: Conceptual Foundations*, lays the theoretical groundwork while the second, *Leadership in the Canadian Forces: Doctrine*, succinctly captures what it means to be an effective leader within the Navy, Army, and Air Force elements of the Canadian Forces. Although it is beyond the scope of this chapter to recreate the rationale for the approach to leadership that has been espoused, it is important to note that the adopted definition of leadership is a natural extension of the profession of arms. Specifically, we define leadership as: **directing, motivating, and enabling others to accomplish the mission professionally and ethically, while developing or improving capabilities that contribute to mission success.** This values-based definition of leadership contributes to CF effectiveness as illustrated in Figure 2 below. Within this model, mission success is conceptualized as the primary outcome with external adaptability, internal integration, and member well-being and commitment serving as enabling outcomes. Even though these outcomes are not labelled as "primary" their role is every bit as critical as mission success because effectiveness will not occur if these aspects are ignored.

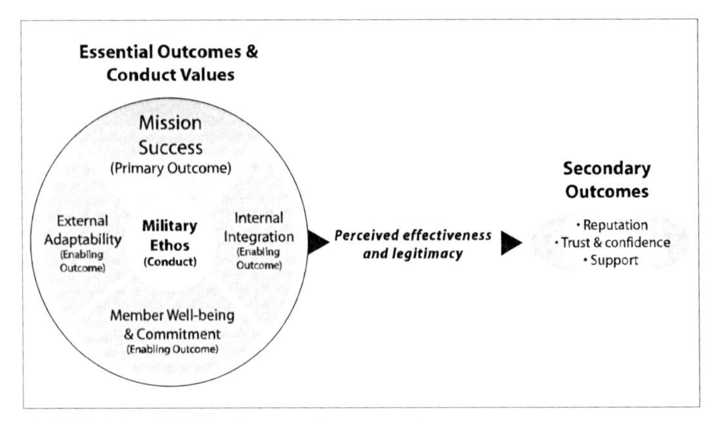

FIGURE 2: CF Effectiveness Framework

Nestled at the core of the essential outcomes is Military ethos. This aspect, which ensures that we conduct ourselves honourably while we carry out our responsibilities, is fully explained within the doctrine related to the profession of arms (*Duty With Honour*). The CF effectiveness framework itself was derived, in part, from Robert Quinn's competing values model of organizational effectiveness.[1] The essential outcomes contained in the framework are conceptualized as being in a continuous state of tension and conflict. This means that leaders have to be constantly aware of these tensions and strive to achieve a meaningful balance.

The secondary outcomes, on the right hand side of the model, are an acknowledgement to the fact that we, as a military force, must operate within the direction and functional responsibilities assigned by the Government. Equally crucial in this equation are Canadian society's expectations of the CF as a national institution. While the expectations of the Government are explicitly contained in legislation, policies, and Cabinet direction, the expectations of Canadian society tend to be implicit. Furthermore, it is

[1] Robert E. Quinn, *Beyond Rational Management: Mastering the Paradoxes and Competing Demands of High Performance* (San Francisco: Josey-Bass, 1988).

important that we never forget that the link between the essential outcomes and the secondary outcomes is phrased as "perceived effectiveness and legitimacy." Given that portrayals of the military in media are, on occasion, sensationalized versions of actual events, perceptions are reality. Perceptions are also prone to be even more polarized when societal expectations are not met. This is a critical aspect of the framework, because the public's trust and confidence in, and support for, the CF should always be a concern for military leaders.

Figure 3 provides an illustration of how the various components of leadership work in harmony to produce the essential outcomes covered by the CF effectiveness model. Leadership is exercised as an influence process that can be either direct or indirect in nature. This model, which is based on Gary Yukl's Multiple-Linkage Model of leadership and group effectiveness,[2] also factors in aspects such as leader characteristics, personal and position power, group characteristics, and situational and environmental factors.

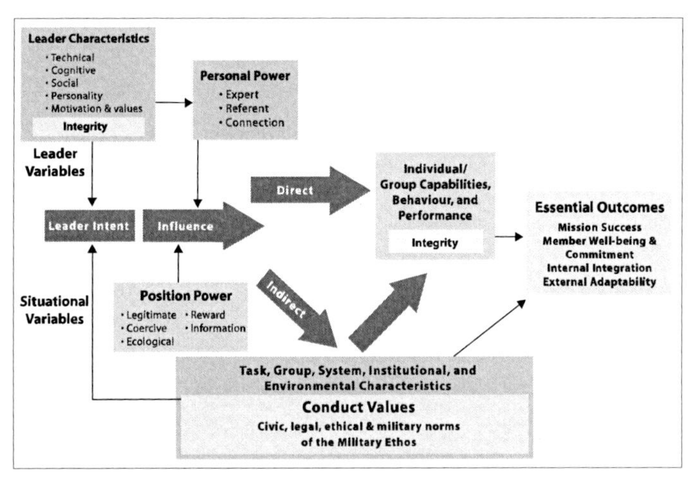

FIGURE 3: Canadian Forces Leadership Model

[2] Gary Yulk, *Leadership In Organizations 5th Edition* (Upper Saddle River, NJ: Prentice-Hall, 2002).

There is one final aspect of this leadership model that should be addressed; specifically, the difference between direct and indirect leadership. There is a widespread assumption that leadership is primarily involved with a face-to-face or direct influence on followers and on performance. In fact, the extant literature on leadership is replete with the behaviours of managers, leaders, and supervisors who are primarily engaged in conducting organizational activities. Earlier in this chapter, it was mentioned that CFLI would soon be publishing doctrine on leading people and leading the institution. It would be easy to confuse "direct" leadership with "leading people" and "indirect" leadership with "institutional leadership," but this is not the case.

Both lower and upper level leaders in an organization may exercise direct leadership and indirect leadership. The essential difference between the two is a matter of closeness between leaders and followers and the time required for leaders to have an effect. Direct leadership is unmediated and fast acting. Conversely, indirect leadership is a mediated process and it can have two kinds effects on behaviour and performance. First, it can have an impact on the slower but longer-term changes in the beliefs and values of subordinates and, second, it can effect changes to the task and organizational conditions that influence behaviour and performance. This can include features such as training and development programs, technology, organizational structure, reward systems, policies and operating procedures. In summary, we can lead people either directly or indirectly and, similarly, we can engage in institutional leadership in either an indirect or direct manner. This notion is captured in Figure 4 below. Although it is evident that leading people occurs most often at lower rank levels, and is primarily a direct influence, there is an overlap in these characteristics. The influence at lower rank levels can also be indirect in nature. Similarly, those at higher rank levels can both lead people and exercise institutional leadership, and this can be either a direct or indirect influence.

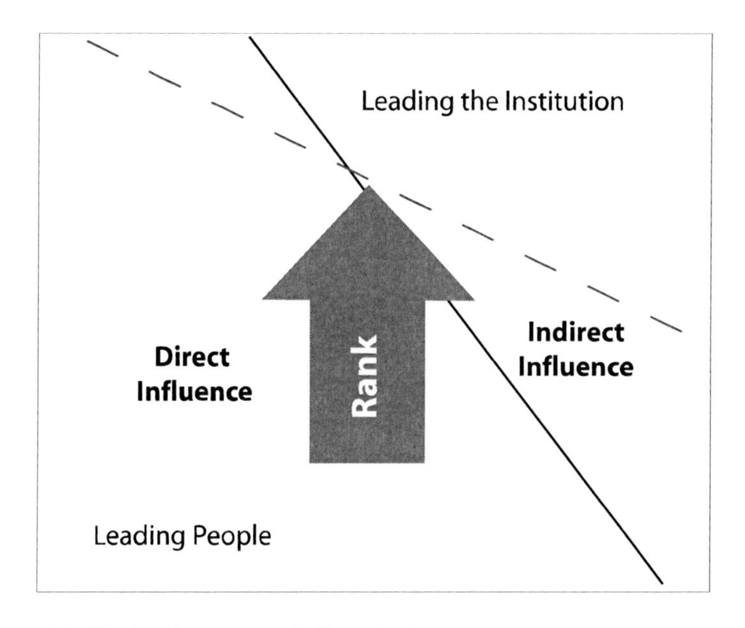

FIGURE 4: Direct versus Indirect Influence.

The recently published CF leadership doctrine also contains twelve principles of leadership, drawn from experience. They cover the major dimensions of effectiveness, and can be viewed as an introduction to the responsibilities of leadership. These principles are:

1. Achieve professional competence and pursue self-improvement;

2. Clarify objectives and intent;

3. Solve problems and make timely decisions;

4. Direct; motivate by persuasion and example and by sharing risks and hardships;

5. Train individuals and teams under demanding and realistic conditions;

6. Build teamwork and cohesion;

7. Keep subordinates informed; explain events and decisions;

8. Mentor, educate, and develop subordinates;

9. Treat subordinates fairly; respond to their concerns; represent their interests;

10. Maintain situational awareness; seek information; keep current;

11. Learn from experience and those who have experience; and,

12. Exemplify and reinforce the military ethos; maintain order and discipline; uphold professional norms.

The definitions, models, frameworks, and principles espoused in the preceding section can be captured in the statement that effective CF leaders get the job done, look after their people, think and act in terms of the larger team, anticipate and adapt to change, and exemplify the military ethos in all that they do.

Remaining Challenges

The establishment of a military leadership institute does not occur without a growing pain or two. Some of the initial challenges are still ongoing, while others have cropped up during the intervening years. There is no doubt that the future will hold additional, currently unanticipated, challenges:

Rigid Mindsets. One ongoing issue is related to the need to encourage military leaders to think of leadership in new, and sometimes innovative, ways. Militaries have a long tradition of authoritarian, autocratic, and transactional approaches to leadership. The notion that military leadership can also be transformational is one that is often met with resistance from some stalwarts of the old approaches. Those who adopt the stance that "if it ain't broke, don't fix it," can be immutable in their resolve to continue to approach leadership in a manner that generates the least amount of discomfort. Rule-based leadership continues to be at odds with values/principle-based leadership.

Denial. On a similar tact, military personnel, particularly the combat arms, often have a very arrogant perspective on leadership. First, they deny that there is a leadership problem – often holding up reported digressions as the results of a "few bad apples," the negative reporting, sensationalism of the media or just down right inaccurate information. Secondly, they believe that they have nothing to learn since they practice leadership on a daily basis. Moreover, they conduct operations and lead individuals in harm's way, and therefore, find it unfathomable that there is something about leadership they do not know or understand. As such, there is sometimes a resistance to new leadership doctrine or concepts.

The Crisis is Over. Inter-related with the previous two points, the serious problems of the 1990s are long passed. The institution has reformed itself and has re-earned the respect and trust of its government and society. At present, it has never been more highly regarded and its personnel are seen as consummate professionals. As such, particularly when there are budgetary pressures, the need for professional development and the associated organizations are often the first to be considered for cost savings. "What 'value added' do they represent?" is often the rationale put forward.

Publicity/Awareness. Since the establishment of CFLI, the institute has published doctrine, leadership books, DVDs and videos, and launched a website. Its members have travelled the country to provide lectures on leadership and professionalism. Yet, we still encounter serving members with blank stares when we declare that we are from CFLI. Although we are making efforts to network extensively, and are being as proactive as possible to spread the word, our efforts to communicate our existence have not always been successful. Ironically, there is a growing awareness that we are almost better known internationally than we are in our own country.

Command and Control. When discussions about establishing a CF leadership institute were originally entertained, one thought was that the institute should report directly to the Chief of the Defence Staff (CDS). It was then decided that CFLI would report to the Assistant Deputy Minister Human Resources Military (ADM (HR Mil)), a Lieutenant-General. With the establishment of the Canadian Defence Academy, an agency with responsibility for all common CF training and education, a decision was made for CFLI to report to the Commander CDA (a Major-General). While this is a natural fit, it does introduce a lower level of operational autonomy, places the institute one step further away from the CDS, and means that CFLI becomes more like another HQ Directorate than an institute in the way in which it must operate.

Mandate. Associated with the above point is the confusion that seems to exist with respect to the CFLI mandate. Because CFLI is now part of CDA, and CDA is responsible for all common education and training, there is an assumption that CFLI must, by extension, be responsible for leadership education and training. Although the doctrine produced by CFLI provides educational material that is introduced to the system, this is not the case. Members of CFLI are also constantly explaining that our mandate extends beyond the publication of the initial run of leadership and professionalism doctrine. There seems to be a perception that, once the next couple of doctrinal manuals are published, our job will be complete and there will no longer be a reason for CFLI to exist. This is also not the case.

Budget. There are those who view CFLI with envy because the assigned budget appears to be large for such a small organization. This leads to an ongoing effort to explain that the work CFLI engages in is expensive by nature. Publishing is a costly endeavour, as are video production, networking efforts (e.g., conferences, working groups), contracting, and translations. In addition to attending relevant conferences, CFLI plans, organizes, and conducts several conferences, workshops, and seminars every year.

Operational Focus. Another challenge is ensuring the institute remains rooted to an operational focus. Too often, an overly academic research orientation creeps in with a mindset that research be conducted for the sake of research or to further personal interests or career aspirations. Military and civilian members must be made to stay focused on the mission of "supporting the generation of effective military leaders." Any and all projects must be advanced with the aim and outcome of assisting military and civilian defence employees of becoming more effective, particularly on operations.

Staff Qualifications. CFLI is primarily a think tank. This means that it must be staffed with highly qualified (i.e., Master's degrees and PhDs) members from a wide variety of academic disciplines. This is important both in terms of credibility and in terms of effective contributions to the work that CFLI produces. Unfortunately, military personnel who have completed advanced degrees are scarce. This means that the institute must rely upon qualified civilian members to ensure that appropriate academic standards are maintained. This, in and of itself, is not a bad thing, but there is also a desire for the people at CFLI to have a strong grasp of military matters. This is not always readily available in civilian applicants for CFLI positions.

Future Direction – The Way Ahead

CFLI has mapped out a future that includes research, publishing, doctrinal work, and continual input into the educational and training system. All of the doctrine manuals will continue to be reviewed for currency and accuracy, updated regularly, and republished in a timely manner. The CF will never again be forced to wait three decades for a new version of its leadership manuals. Research will be directed at ensuring that the models and theories postulated in our manuals are borne out in operational realities and will also explore aspects of leadership that have not been previously considered. We will achieve our vision to become "a national centre of excellence for leadership and professionalism research, concept development and doctrine." We recognize that any recognition as a centre of excellence must come from outside the institute and we will become known by our actions, reputation, and scholastic achievements.

CHAPTER 3

Strategic Leadership Education

Air Commodore Peter W. Gray and Jonathan Harvey

Leadership is one of the most observed and least understood phenomena on earth.[1]

James MacGregor Burns

Despite the plethora of works published on leadership, the truth behind Burns' statement remains extant today. Trying to grasp the basics, let alone the subtleties, of leadership is made all the more complex by virtue of everyone having a view on the subject. The more senior the officer – or civil servant – the more convinced they are that their perceptions are the most authoritative. Strategic leadership education is further bedevilled by the reluctance of many to accept that leadership education is a lifelong journey through which we all can learn. The well-known precept that leadership can be learned – but not taught – should be taken as a given in this process. In the ideal world, officers, warrant officers, senior non-commissioned officers and the troops would embark on a coherent thread of leadership development that would see them through their entire careers. If anything, this perfect process is actually impeded by initiatives and well-meaning bright ideas.

The challenge is made all the greater as the single-Services remain, very properly, determined to mould their young officers and new recruits and instil them with the ethos of their profession. The appropriate level at which a joint, or purple, organisation can be allowed to work on the attitudes, values and beliefs of service personnel and officials is problematic to say the least. All that said, the traditional

---

[1] James MacGregor Burns, *Leadership* (New York: Harper, 1979), 2.

approach to leadership education and development across the three Services in the United Kingdom shows more in common than any radical diversions.

Leadership Development in a Historical Context

A historical review of leadership development is inevitably plagued by the difficulty of knowing when to start. It is also challenging to apply contemporary notions of leadership education in an earlier context where the common vocabulary differed markedly; this is often compounded by a reluctance to commit views to the files that would end up in archives. One can accept a general progression from the Ancients with glib quotations from Plato into manifestations of Great Man Theory from Alexander the Great onwards[2]. It would, however, be more meaningful from a British perspective, but controversially from a Commonwealth view point, to start at the beginning of the 20th Century and the experience of the Great War.

In his work *Leadership in the Trenches*,[3] Professor Gary Sheffield highlights the generally low standard of education, health and social standing of the average soldier – who had probably joined under 'the compulsion of hunger'.[4] The officer cadre had traditionally been taken from families with military tradition in their lineage, the landed gentry, the peerage and, to a lesser extent from the professions and the clergy. Their educational pedigree was entirely predictable – they had all attended the better known public schools (it should be noted for those not familiar with British nomenclature that a public

[2] See for example, Manfred Kets de Vries, "Doing an Alexander: Lessons on Leadership by a Master Conqueror," *European Management Journal*, Vol 21, No 3, June 2003, 370-375.

[3] G. D. Sheffield, *Leadership in the Trenches: Officer-Man Relations, Morale, and Discipline in the British Army in the era of the First World War* (London: Macmillan, 2000).

[4] Ibid., 1.

school is one that charges fees – state schools do not). Leadership was effectively learned on the playing fields of these establishments or in the routine business of managing one's estate and seeing to the well-being of one's workers.

Professor Sheffield confirms what most contemporary readers would intuitively infer, that inter-rank relations within Dominion formations were looser and more informal.[5] Not surprisingly, the casualty rates of the early years of World War I had a serious effect of this traditional source of supply and the British Army had to look elsewhere. As the War progressed, greater numbers of men were commissioned from the ranks and officers were recruited from a wider cross-section of society. Ironically, greater numbers of those from the middle-classes also swelled the other-ranks. As Sheffield points out, the balance between paternalism and harsh discipline was more-or-less maintained, albeit that the influx of thinking men into the ranks tended to mean that the harshness was less appropriate.[6]

The end of the War, and ensuing demobilisations, brought about an entirely predictable return to the old ways until the Second World War required the whole to be revisited. Again, the shortage of suitable candidates for officer cadet training was identified. With failure rates through Officer Cadet Training Units as high as 50 percent, the British Army set about trying to identify a scientific methodology by which officers could be selected on the basis of their leadership potential – rather than just by interview.[7] By 1945, the War Office Selection Board processes had matured to the point that they were being adopted by the other Services and into wider organisations where leadership potential was critical. The team looked at leadership in many guises, but they

5 Ibid, 166.

6 Ibid, 178.

7 Henry Harris, *The Group Approach to Leadership Testing* (London: Routledge, 1949).

identified, as a recurring theme, that the leadership function could be looked at in three important aspects – the team, the individual and task. Leadership was therefore a functional relationship between these three basic variables.[8]

The evident success of the testing regime, at least in the Army and the Royal Air Force, was such that it was left in place after the end of the War, and indeed remains the foundation for testing in the Services today. Leadership education tended to remain relatively in the doldrums with inevitable reliance on the Ancients and Great Man theory. Although the Royal Military Academy at Sandhurst (RMAS) and the Britannia Royal Naval College at Dartmouth (BRNC) had full academic departments, the RAF College at Cranwell did not. The mould was broken in the mid-sixties with the research carried out by Dr. John Adair who developed the principles that underpinned the testing into a comprehensive theory of functional leadership.[9] Adair has subsequently published widely on the basis of functional leadership with the three variables of team, task and individual needs being represented in a Venn diagram with the size of each circle depending on the context at hand. From a training perspective, Adair broke down the functions further into setting objectives, briefing, planning, controlling, informing, supporting and reviewing. This methodology allowed for cadets, from all three Services, to analyse their performance in a range of exercises not dissimilar to those originally envisaged for the testing arena. The Adair approach is in use today in a wide variety of institutions and organisations. Interestingly, it is not widely cited with, for example, only one reference to Adair and action-centred leadership in Bass & Stogdill.[10]

---

[8] Ibid., 19.

[9] See Dr. J. E. Adair, "New Trends in Leadership and Management Training," based on a lecture give in Royal United Services Institute (RUSI) on 19 April 1967 and subsequently published in the Journal of the RUSI that year.

[10] Bernard M Bass, *Bass & Stogdill's Handbook of Leadership: Theory, Research and Managerial Implications*, Third Edition (New York: Free Press, 1981), 384.

This throws up an interesting divergence amongst leadership theorists with separate camps being occupied by the behavioural psychologists, sociologists, military historians and the business school world. Presumably this could easily be reflected in an appropriate two-by-two! Suffice it to say, the behavioural psychologists do not consider there to have been sufficient methodological rigour in Adair's work for it to be relevant. Adair himself, is absolutely unabashed stating, in several discussions with authors, that his work has more than stood the test of time.[11]

The end of the Cold War (which seems to get the blame for a lot of things) coincided, in the UK at least, with a desire to make as many institutions joint as possible. The individual Services balked at any notion of combining initial officer training but eventually acceded to a Joint Command and Staff College with the Advanced and Higher courses being truly purple. These have been running successfully for some nine years. With increasing emphasis of deployed operations, and the need to be able to operate within combined operations centres, has seen the emphasis shift to operational art, campaign planning and the generations of skills necessary to function as a component commander – or member of his staff.[12] The concomitant decline in traditional staff skills came at a time when a number of studies – including across government – were concluding that inadequate provision was being made in the field of public sector management and strategic leadership.

---

[11] See the article by Sue Weeks, "Professor versus Professor," *Edge* (the Journal of the Institute of Leadership and Management), September 2005, 24–27 in which Adair debates the state of leadership education in the United Kingdom with Professor Keith Grint (formerly of the Universities of Oxford and Lancaster who takes up the Chair of Defence Leadership with Cranfield University with the Defence Leadership & Management Centre at Shrivenham)

[12] One of the authors, Air Commodore Peter Gray, was Assistant Director of the 2001 Higher Command and Staff Course and is a graduate of the programme.

The Formation of the Defence Leadership Centre

Following the election of the Labour government in 1997, the Modernising Government initiative of the Prime Minister (White Paper 1999) sought to examine the role of the public services. As part of this process, the role of leadership in the public services came under scrutiny, resulting in the establishment of a number of centres with the mandate to develop leadership within their respective sectors. This included centres for the National Health Service and Higher Education. The Defence Training Review (DTR) recognised that "operational leadership skills are amongst the Armed Forces' most valuable assets" and that those demonstrated on recent operations were "acknowledged as being amongst the best in the world" it nevertheless recognised the need to "meet the demand for improved leadership skills". Further clarifying work led to Ministers' agreement to the establishment of the Defence Leadership Centre (DLC) in 2002 as part of the wider Defence Academy.

Defence Context

The view held within defence and endorsed by the DTR is that through our range of training and development opportunities in both the single service and joint environments, we equip our military leaders to lead in operations with a high degree of effectiveness. The challenge that we face is that for much of an individual's career (both military and civilian) their leadership will be tested in non-operational roles. What has been termed 'The Business Space' (in contrast to 'The Battle Space'). Whilst one might take issue with the terms, arguing that perhaps equipment development / acquisition for example is simply a less immediate form of Battle Space, particularly if you consider where the consequences of failure to deliver may be felt, the distinction serves to illustrate the need to consider the leadership roles that military and civilian leaders in the business of defence.

Within UK Defence, as with many organisations, the move into strategic leadership is a critical one. From the perspective of the individual, this may be the first time in their career that they have had to take a view beyond their particular service or specialty. This transition should not be underestimated in terms of the challenges that result. It means an individual must move from a career that to date has focused on perhaps regimental or specialist skills to one that embraces the broader issues for defence. This is a large step change in perspective. The challenge of setting and selling the future direction of the organisation beyond single-Service aspirations undoubtedly will result in difficult decisions and conflicts of interest.

All this to say that the development of an officer's career in which the emphasis is on the operational is insufficient to equip them for the wider challenges that are likely to be faced at the strategic level of defence. From the perspective of the civil service, a career that has been characterised by the ability to develop and implement policy, and effectively run the administrative functions of defence is also an insufficient basis for addressing the organisational challenges that are present at the strategic level. In both cases, the demands of operating on defence boards and executive committees provide a number of challenges.

In light of the seriousness of the challenges facing those at the strategic level of defence, it is clear that Defence has an obligation to provide the language, concepts and skills that equip them to deliver the strategic role. The challenges in the business of defence are significant and should not be underestimated, specific consideration therefore of the development needs of these individuals lies at the heart of the Defence Leadership and Management Centre (DLMC).

Whilst there is a general acceptance of the need to support senior staff in the delivery of the strategic role, there is less of a consensus on the detail of what should be developed. Often the expression is of the need to 'improve leadership' which on closer inspection may lead to a wide variety of development and structural/organisational issues, after all, leadership development should not be seen as a panacea for all ills. Indeed, the development of the leadership centre into a leadership and management centre reflects the holistic approach being advocated by the Academy. Closer examination reveals it is indeed entirely possible that the barriers to success at a particular level lay in organisational or structural failings, not leadership or management deficits.

Mission

The DLC was established in 2002 with the remit to "improve leadership in defence," "at the strategic level" and "beyond the domain of war-fighting." The strategic level was defined in terms of rank (i.e. one-star general rank level and above) with the single services and civil service retaining responsibility for leadership development up to that point. This reflected the desire of the single-Services to retain their particular leadership culture and context in the development of officers with the civil service utilising its existing development tracks.

The initial task of the DLC was the establishment of a Strategic Leadership Programme for newly appointed one-star general rank officers or senior civil servants that would run four times a year capturing the average annual appointment to that level. Key stakeholders in this programme were the Vice Chief of the Defence Staff, the 2nd Permanent Undersecretary of Defence and the Director of the Defence Academy. The DLC was also tasked with providing definitions of Command, Leadership and Management.

'One-Star' Rank Survey

The initial challenge in this undertaking was to ask what it is that we mean by strategic leadership in UK Defence. Unless we could articulate a view of leadership that was broadly recognisable to those at the strategic level of defence and presented in such a way that a programme could be built around it then the achievement of our first objective, the establishment of the one-star general's course, would be extremely difficult to say the least.

This resulted in a piece of research that involved a survey of the entire one star population of UK Defence with the aim of establishing how that population viewed the nature of leadership at the strategic level. The survey was followed by a series of in-depth interviews with a sample of that population using repertory grid and critical incident methodology.

Development of helix model

A literature review was undertaken in order to understand the evolution of leadership theory underpinning contemporary thought in order to inform judgments on the validity of current leadership definitions and models. On the assumption, supported by the literature, that leadership is culturally contextual,[13] a survey was undertaken of thirteen UK-based organisations across Defence, the wider Civil Service, the public sector, the private sector and academia. The US Army was included as a fourteenth organisation in order to broaden the sample, however it remained within a separate cultural cluster and military context. The attributes, qualities, competencies, values and actions ascribed to by these organisations where compared and analysed to extract the most frequently cited attributes.[14] This produced a model of six broadly clustered attributes; Integrity, Vision, Communication, Decision Taking, Innovation, and Focused on Development. In order to reflect both ancient[15] and modern[16] thinking on ideals of leadership excellence, Humility was included despite scoring poorly.

[13] B.M. Bass, *Bass & Stogdill's Handbook of Leadership. 3rd Edition* (New York: The Free Press, 1990), 760-803.

[14] Attribute was adopted as the most appropriate generic term embracing the different descriptors used across the fourteen organisations surveyed.

[15] J. Adair, *Effective Strategic Leadership* (London: Macmillan, 2002), 103-109.

[16] J. Collins, *Good To Great* (London: Random House, 2001).

Following compilation of the initial survey results, a facilitated 'stakeholder' workshop was held for four senior people representing the Royal Navy, Army and Royal Air Force Boards and the Ministry of Defence (MOD) Civil Service, to consider what outcomes they would seek in a Strategic Leadership Programme. This event endorsed the attributes identified and highlighted the (perceived) importance of professional knowledge and a thorough understanding of the environment in which senior leaders operate. It led to the addition of 'Professional Knowledge' to the model, to ensure it fulfilled their aspirations. The resulting model is represented in Figure 1. The representation of the DNA double helix was used to illustrate the model as it represents the manner in which the attributes combine to create the unique leadership of an individual. The hydrogen bonds that hold the helix together represent self-awareness underpinning the development of effective leadership. The question mark represents the uniqueness of the individual.

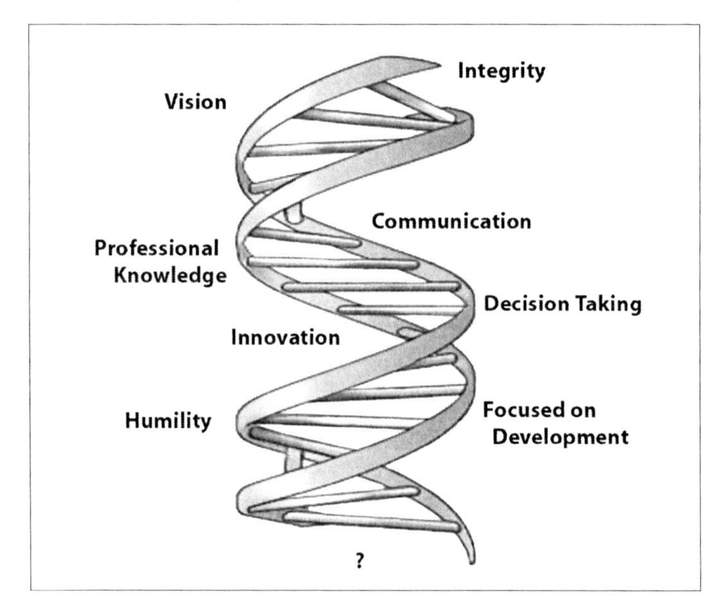

FIGURE 1: The Defence helix Model

Definitions

Given the abundance of writing on the subject of leadership and management, the wide variety of definitions and the requirement to provide definitions for UK Defence, this rather daunting task was undertaken with a very clear view to the context in which leaders must operate in the UK. They are presented here for reference, not as a statement that we have the definitive answer.

Command *is a position of authority and responsibility to which military men and women are legally appointed. Leadership and management are the key components to the successful exercise of Command. Successful management is readily measured against objective criteria but commanders are not leaders until their position has been ratified in the hearts and minds of those they command.*

Leadership *is visionary; it is the projection of personality and character to inspire the team to achieve the desired outcome. There is no prescription for leadership and no prescribed style of leader. Leadership is a combination of example, persuasion and compulsion dependent on the situation. It should aim to transform and be underpinned by individual skills and an enabling ethos. The successful leader is an individual who understands him/herself, the organisation, the environment in which they operate and the people that they are privileged to lead.*

Management *is the allocation and control of resources (human, material and financial) to achieve objectives, often within the constraints of time. Management requires the capability to deploy a range of techniques and skills to enhance and facilitate the planning, organization and execution of the business'.* [17]

Development of the Defence Strategic Leadership Programme (DSLP)

The development of the (DSLP) followed from the initial work outlined above. The helix model provided for a framework of

[17] All definitions are copyright DLC.

attributes around which to build a programme. The approach adopted was not to seek to produce a training package, but rather to provide a forum for experienced leaders to reflect on their leadership, the challenges of the strategic level and contemporary leadership thinking. The underlying theme of the programme was to be one of self-awareness and the importance of developing that critical capacity as a vehicle for personal development. For many delegates, this would be the first time in many years, if indeed ever, that they had experienced this approach to development. There was to be no reporting on or assessment of delegates. The structure of the programme was to be a one-week residential phase followed by a number of electives.

As a support to the development of self-awareness, a number of psychological tools were identified, the use of 360-degree feedback was endorsed and the use of the Myers Briggs Type Indicator (a personality type tool) and the Thomas Kilmann Conflict Mode Instrument were adopted. The 360-degree tool was a specially made instrument built around the leadership attributes of the helix model.

A great deal of consideration was given to the mechanisms for delivering this element of the programme. The use of psychological tools, particularly 360, was not common in the UK military and there was some resistance to the proposal. Using a third party organisation to administer, report and feedback the results of the instruments mitigated these concerns, effectively ring fencing the process from any defence involvement. The sole intention in this process is to provide the individual with information.

Discussion of the application and value of self-awareness approaches and the individual feedback of results forms the initial phase of the DSLP providing the foundation for the subsequent sessions that explore issues such as Contemporary Leadership Paradigms, Ethics, Leading Change, Leadership Derailment, Strategy, Followership and the Psychophysiology of leadership. In addition, a day is spent with executives from an organisation outside of defence exploring the strategic challenges that impact both.

The programme includes presentations from both civilian and military four-star general rank members of the Defence Management Board (current and recently retired) to provide insight into the strategic challenges faced at the very highest levels of defence. The ongoing commitment of these individuals has proved invaluable in demonstrating the importance that is attached to the programme.

Following the week residential portion of the programme, a series of electives are available to alumni over the subsequent eighteen months. These electives cover a wide range of areas, typically over a one or two-day period. They include areas such as negotiation skills, working with the media, application of coaching skills, corporate governance, board membership, etc. They are made up of bespoke courses and public access programmes and, where necessary, the centre will design, commission or source an elective to meet a particular individual's needs.

Recent developments to the programme include the option of a further coaching session with the same facilitator from the residential phase 6-8 weeks after completing the residential component. The aim is to provide the opportunity and focus for reflection on the implementation and embedding of learning/insight from the residential phase.

Growth into the DLMC

As the DLC developed the DSLP and associated electives, the requirement to provide for the range of executive development needs became increasingly self-evident. This gave rise to the expansion of the DLC into the DLMC in 2004. This involved the recruitment of staff to mirror those dedicated to leadership development, and in addition, incorporated the existing Defence School Financial Management. This has had the effect of creating a broad organisation with a remit to provide executive education across the range of leadership and management themes. Within this is consideration of the term strategic as a function of role rather than as a function of rank. That is, recognising that there are those below the rank of one-star who nevertheless occupy strategic roles.

Whilst the DSLP is undoubtedly the flagship programme of the DLMC, the engagement of this group of leaders in defence and the growing profile of the organisation has resulted in a wider range of activities being undertaken. This has included the provision of advice and support to other defence organisations in the development of training and support initiatives, and a range of specific interventions including the following.

Master Classes

A programme of master classes has been undertaken for two and three-star general leaders in defence responsible for major change programmes. These are designed to provide a vehicle for discussion on issues such as risk, benefits realisation, governance and leading as a single point of accountability on large change or acquisition programmes.

Defence Leadership Network (DLN)

The DLN is a regular forum for those involved and interested in leadership development in defence and the wider public services, plus invited guests from voluntary organisations and the private sector. A theme is adopted for each network event (up to three a year) with invited speakers presenting different perspectives on that theme. The objective is to expose delegates to a wide range of contemporary issues that pertain to leadership development whilst providing an opportunity for the exchange of ideas and experiences. Recent events have covered themes such as Ethics, Leadership Derailment, Change Leadership and the Physiology of Leadership.

Executive Coaching

The DLMC is the focal point in defence for executive coaching, building contacts and relationships with individuals and organisations providing coaching services and facilitating the provision of coaching for those senior leaders in defence who wish to explore its utility in enhancing performance.

Coaching Network

The coaching network is a forum for those in defence involved in training and development where they can discuss the application of coaching and coaching techniques. This forum, whilst in its early stages, has addressed issues of developing common understanding of terms and techniques and challenges in demonstrating utility.

Board Development

This has involved the DLMC identifying appropriate board level diagnostics and interventions reflecting the unique nature of boards in the defence context. Allied to this has been the process of identifying appropriate sources of support to deliver agreed interventions.

Introduction of Academic Staff on a long term Contract

The Defence Academy of the UK has entered into a long-term contract for the provision of academic services to the Defence College of Management and Technology of which the DLMC is a part. In practice, this means the introduction of a Professor of Leadership, a Senior Lecturer in Management and a Senior Lecturer in Leadership to commence in October 2006. All these appointments are to be research active, contributing to the evidence based underpinning of the DLMC output. It is anticipated that this will include doctoral level research students who will yet further enhance the research base of the DLMC.

Challenge

As the DLMC develops, there are a number of challenges that we must embrace as we continue to improve the delivery of our service. As with many aspects of development, one of the principle challenges lies in the linking of theory to practice. By nature, the armed services have an action orientation and a limited attention span for theory. It is therefore incumbent on the Centre to seek to provide the bridge between the academic and the applied, to translate the theoretical and research base into development opportunities that our population will engage with. The development of the DLMC to include subject matter experts is part of this continuum

Every year, we are told that financial resources are tighter than ever. We have every reason to believe this to be the case for the next two years. Here we have a classic Catch 22 situation in which we need to invest in the education of our people at the highest levels if we are to make best use of the resources. And yet we are constrained ourselves in terms of people and money. Nor are we any different from the rest of Defence – or indeed the rest of the public sector. The critical challenge, therefore, is to design, and implement, a coherent suite of educational and training offerings aimed at meeting the most urgent needs of leaders and decision makers at the higher levels of defence. We are increasingly confident that our aim is becoming increasingly accurate and that the effects of the interventions both relevant and beneficial.

We are also confident that our blend of original research, distilled reasoning and pragmatic approach to learning is paying dividends beyond the immediate remit. Organising events through the Leadership (and Management networks); upcoming major conferences and participating in a range of network events in the public and private sectors have had a disproportionate impact on target audiences.

CHAPTER 4

Leadership 24-7: The Singapore Armed Forces Centre of Leadership Development

Colonel Sukhmohinder Singh,
Lieutenant-Colonel Kim-Yin Chan, PhD and Kwee-Hoon Lim

> *The operational readiness of the SAF may not make headlines everyday. But the SAF is constantly at work quietly behind the scenes – whether conducting regular naval and air patrols in the Malacca Straits, securing our major international events like the International Olympic meeting, or escorting high value ships through our sea lanes.*[1]

The Singapore Armed Forces (SAF) has come a long way since its creation at the birth of our Nation about 40 years ago. In 1965, newly independent Singapore was highly vulnerable with a total defence capability that only consisted of two under-strength battalions, of which only half the soldiers were Singaporeans. With limited resources, we had to rely on a system of universal conscription to build up our defence capability. Today, the SAF is a tri-service force comprised of about 350,000 operationally ready soldiers, equipped with the most modern technologies and hardware, and trained to operate with the highest standards of professionalism.

While its core mission remains the defence of Singapore's sovereignty and territorial integrity, the SAF has also initiated efforts to transform itself to better deal with a wider spectrum of threats and operations other than war. What began as a

[1] Statement by Minister of Defence, Mr. Teo Chee Hean at the *Committee of Supply Debate*, 7 March 2006.

series of limited medical or observer/adviser peace-support roles in the 1990s (e.g., Namibia in 1989, Kuwait from 1991 to 2003, Angola in 1991/1992, Cambodia in 1992/1993, Afghanistan in 1997/1998) culminated in a larger scale, 370-strong medical and logistics support force that was sent as part of a United Nations (UN) sanctioned international force called International Force East Timor (INTERFET; led by Australia) to stabilize a crisis situation in East Timor. This support evolved into a UN peacekeeping operation, the United Nations Transitional Administration in East Timor (UNTAET), that aimed to stabilize the transition of East Timor to independence from 2000 to 2002. In this, its first deployment of armed peacekeepers, the SAF deployed up to a company-sized force of troops in Timor Leste.

Singapore was not spared when the world faced up to the threat of global terrorism on September 2001. Soon after the attacks on the World Trade Center in the U.S., Singapore's security agencies uncovered a plot by global terrorists to blow up several prominent structures on our island. Nor were many of our neighboring countries spared. For example, there have been several terrorist bombings in Bali and Jakarta since 2002 targeting both the Indonesian locals and the foreign visitors.

In recent years, the SAF has maintained a high operational tempo in humanitarian and disaster relief operations. For example, after assisting in the post-tsunami humanitarian and disaster relief operation in Aceh and Meulaboh, Indonesia in early 2005, the SAF deployed its forces again to assist in an earthquake that struck off the Indonesian island of Nias in March. The SAF also assisted when Hurricane Katrina struck New Orleans in August 2005. In October that year, two SAF C-130s delivered aid to Pakistan after an earthquake hit parts of the country.

Today, SAF not only has to deal with any conventional threats that may arise, our soldiers also work hand-in-hand with our homeland defence forces (including police and civil defence forces) to protect our key national assets like our international airport and our key industries and oil refineries. More than ever, the SAF is today a "24-7" military force – one that has to maintain a high state of readiness for a wide spectrum of operations 24-hours a day, 7-days a week.

The growing complexity in our security environment has brought about a bigger challenge and a heavier responsibility for all who serve in the SAF. In order to deal with a wider range of new threats and yet stay anchored on its fundamental purpose to defend Singapore, the SAF decided that it needed to equip its leaders with different capabilities and skills, and a different orientation in their mindsets. In 2003, the SAF formally announced its efforts to transform itself into a "Third Generation" or 3G military force – one that would have enhanced capabilities via the exploitation of new concepts and technologies, and, an improved ability to fight across a wider spectrum of operations.[2]

Key to the transformation was a desire to leverage on the high level of education and technological-savvyness that our National Servicemen bring with them into the organization. Hence, besides establishing new structures like a Future Systems Directorate and an SAF Centre for Military Experimentation, the SAF also embarked on an effort to transform its training and education structures, starting with the SAFTI Military Institute[3] where a new SAF Centre of Leadership Development (CLD) was created in 2002.[4] The creation of the Centre was a recognition that the key to harnessing the human potential for the 3G SAF was effective and adaptive leaders who were able to influence their men to operate under the most challenging circumstances and under a wider spectrum of operations.

---

[2] Statement by Minister for Defence, RADM(NS) Teo Chee Hean, at the *Committee of Supply debate*, 15 March 2004.

[3] Note that with the formation of the new Military Institute in 1995, the acronym for "SAF Training Institute" or "SAFTI" is now treated as a word in Singapore.

[4] Speech by Mr Teo Chee Hean, Minister for Defence, at SAFTI MI 10th Anniversary Dinner, 25 August 2005.

Leadership Development in the Early Years

In what is now called its "First Generation" of development from the mid-60s to the late 70s, leadership development in the SAF largely focused on the search and shaping of a military ethos and culture, influenced by the founding concerns of building a basic military capability for Singapore via a National Service system.[5] In its early years, much of the SAF's military culture was shaped by the direct influence of political leaders like Dr. Goh Keng Swee, who felt that the Singapore military could not simply rely on traditions inherited from the British or other forces; that the SAF instead needed its own Code of Conduct that spelled out the unique professional role of the SAF in Singaporean society. "Leadership by Example" was acknowledged as the unwritten doctrine that guided the SAF leaders' thinking on "how to lead" in the SAF. It was not until 1984 that the SAF publicly announced that "Leadership-by-example" was its official leadership philosophy, as part of *The SAF Declaration* that was to act as a "reference document" for the SAF's beliefs and actions.[6]

The period of the SAF's history from the 1980s to the 1990s is today referred to as the second generation or "2G" SAF. If leadership development in the 1G SAF was characterized by a focus on matters of military spirit and ethos, the 2G SAF focused more on the building of leadership development systems and structures. In 1982, then-Singapore-Prime Minister Lee Kuan Yew initiated a move to build a new military institute for the SAF Officer Corps that would be a symbol of service to the Nation. As part of the establishment of SAFTI Military Institute in 1995, the SAF Officer Cadet School worked with behavioral scientists from the Singapore

---

[5] Kim-Yin Chan, Sukhmohinder Singh, Regena Ramaya, and Kwee-Hoon Lim. *Spirit and System: Leadership Development for a Third Generation SAF* (Pointer Monograph No. 4; Singapore: SAFTI Military Institute, 2005), 3.

[6] "The SAF Declaration", *Pointer: Journal of the SAF*, July-September, 1984.

Ministry of Defence (or MINDEF) to derive a leadership framework called the Knowledge, Abilities and Qualities (or KAQ) Model. The effort to envision the concept of "SAFTI Military Institute" in the late-80s also brought to light the need for a set of Core Values that should encapsulate the Values System and "Character" of the SAF. In 1990, the SAF Leadership agreed on a set of seven Core SAF Values, and a decision was made first to infuse these values to the SAF Officer Corps via the articulation of an SAF Officer's Creed, and then to later promulgate the values SAF-wide.

When it was opened in 1995, SAFTI Military Institute published the first (provisional) SAF Leadership Handbook that incorporated both the KAQ Model and the SAF Core Values. Located in the 1995 SAFTI Military Institute Headquarters was a small Leadership Development Branch (LDB) that comprised three military staff officers who were entrusted with the task of "spearheading excellence in leadership development in the SAF". The new SAF Leadership Handbook, drafted by the MINDEF Psychologists, described the knowledge, abilities and qualities expected of the SAF's junior commanders (from section to company level), and also covered topics like "morale", "combat stress" and "cohesion". It was distributed to all junior officers who attended courses in the Institute, and was used to support a new set of "leadership" lessons created by the MINDEF Psychologists but managed by LDB – based on the KAQ model.

In 1996, the SAF finally decided that it was ready to promulgate the seven SAF Core Values to all ranks, vocations and services. SAFTI Military Institute therefore published a new SAF Core Values Guide that was distributed to all new recruits in the SAF. This marked the SAF's readiness to shape its "character" organization-wide. LDB then became the custodian for values education and training beyond SAFTI Military Institute – for all SAFTI Training Schools. This also stretched the resources of the three-man Branch, which continued to rely on MINDEF Psychologists to support the many SAF Schools in the area of leadership development.

New Demands and Enduring Imperatives

By the beginning of the 21st century, the SAF realized that it had to move beyond the inculcation of values and leadership training to respond more effectively to changes in the external environment. In 2001, a call was made by the then-Chief of Defence Lt. Gen. Lim Chuan Poh for SAFTI Military Institute to review the SAF's system of leadership development, and to chart the way forward to better prepare SAF Leaders for the future operating environment. A project group comprising experienced military commanders and military behavioral scientists was formed to develop a new "SAF Leadership Masterplan". Together with LDB, the project group organized a series of senior leadership dialogues from 2002 to 2003 to chart the directions for enhancing the SAF's leadership development system. From these dialogues, two key imperatives were identified for enhancing leadership in the SAF – Mission and People:

- Mission. The SAF recognized that the new battlefield would be characterized by increased levels of volatility, uncertainty, complexity and ambiguity. This battlefield did not have clear lines of conflict, and could not be engaged effectively by merely enhancing military technology. The SAF's expanded spectrum of operations, especially in the face of terrorist threats and other forms of low intensity conflict, meant that leaders and soldiers were now expected to take on new responsibilities beyond what they were traditionally trained for. In order for the leaders to effectively harness the strengths of our fighting men and women, and to make effective use of new technologies, SAF leaders would need to be self-aware and adaptive life-long learners, anchored on the SAF Core Values and committed to the Nation.

- People. The SAF recognized that with changes in Singapore society, SAF servicemen and women, both conscript and regular are becoming increasingly better educated, knowledgeable and discerning. Their leaders would therefore have to possess a wide repertoire of leadership styles and behavioral skills to motivate and bring out the best in them. Such dynamic and flexible leadership is needed to create the positive experiences, continual learning and commitment among our servicemen and women.

A New Definition and Framework

Given the SAF's new social and operational context, the project team proposed to the SAF leadership the need for a wider definition of leadership, viewing it as "a process of influencing people to accomplish the mission, inspiring their commitment and improving the organization". This definition emphasized that leadership is a behavior that can be developed, rather than a feature of rank, personality or position. In contrast with the earlier, "task-focused" definition of leadership in the 1995 SAF Leadership Handbook, the new definition also emphasized the need for leaders not only to influence mission-outcomes, but also to build long-term commitment and to improve the larger organization.

Also endorsed by the SAF leadership in 2002 was a new SAF Leadership framework, now called "SAF Leadership 24-7" (see Figure 1). The new framework emphasizes that leadership training and development must always include two aspects – an understanding of the leadership context and the four domains of leadership development, namely, values, competencies, styles, and self. Along with the three aspects of the leadership context (i.e., mission and purpose, operating environment, and desired outcomes), the new Framework identifies a total of seven components that must be covered as part of the SAF's total leadership development system.

The framework not only expands on the list of "ingredients" for effective leadership articulated in the previous KAQ model, it also emphasizes the importance of the unique, "24-7" context in which SAF leaders are expected to lead:

Today, it is no longer enough just to be operationally ready to fight conventional battles to safeguard Singapore's sovereignty and territorial integrity. Today, and more so than before, the SAF has troops operating 24-hours, 7-days a week at high alert against the threat of global terrorism, working alongside other security forces to safeguard our airport, sea-lanes and key installations. Operating under difficult conditions and facing real dangers and challenges, our soldiers are expected to serve with a high degree of professionalism. Key to their success is the influence of leaders who understand the SAF's mission and purpose, appreciate the operating environment, and who act to achieve the desired outcomes. These must be leaders who act on the basis of the SAF Core Values, are competent and flexible in their leadership styles, and possess the "meta-competency" skills of self-awareness, self-management and personal mastery.[7]

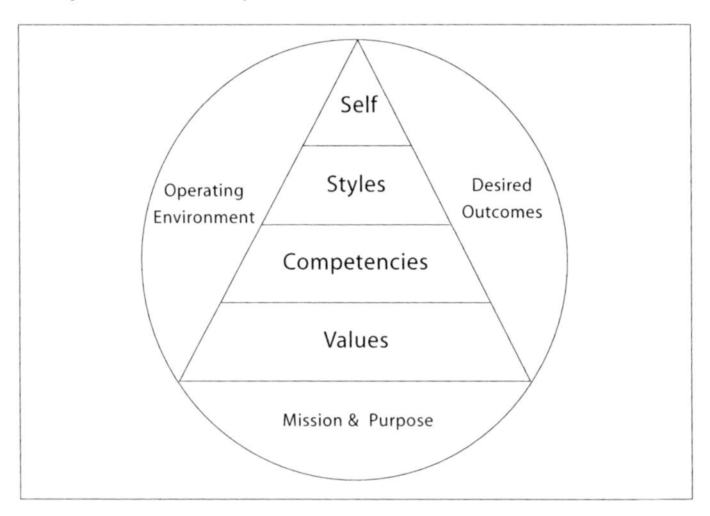

FIGURE 1: "SAF Leadership 24-7": The new SAF Leadership Framework

[7] Kim-Yin Chan and Psalm Lew describe how these four building blocks of leadership in the framework are based on four leadership research traditions or "paradigms" in the behavioral sciences in "The Challenge of Systematic Leadership Development in the SAF", *Pointer: Journal of the Singapore Armed Forces*, 30, no. 4, (2005), 5.

The circle and the triangle above provide a heuristic for thinking and talking about the meaning of leadership in the SAF:

- Triangle ('Building Blocks'). The triangle provides a framework to specify 'what SAF Leaders need' for effective leadership. The hierarchy of 'building blocks' says that values must always form the basic foundation, upon which competencies and a full range of styles are best employed in leadership. The 'Self' (consisting of self-awareness, self-management and personal mastery) is most difficult to attain, and includes a good understanding of one's own values, competencies and styles. The hierarchy does not prescribe a sequence for development or imply that some 'building blocks' are more important than others.

- Circle ('Leadership Context'). The circle emphasizes that SAF Leaders must influence people with a good understanding of the SAF's mission and purpose, the operating environment and desired outcomes. It is these three aspects of the 'leadership context' that shape the specific contents of the framework, i.e., the specific styles, competencies, and values desired in each Service or level of leadership in the SAF.

- Circle and Triangle. Together, the 'building blocks' (triangle) and 'leadership context' (circle) spell-out the scope of concerns of leadership development system in the SAF. In other words, when we think of 'leadership development in the SAF', it includes education and training in the domain of values, competencies, styles and 'self'. All these must be done in cognizance of the mission and purpose of the SAF, its operating environment, and the desired outcomes.

The SAF Centre of Leadership Development

In December 2002, the project group was merged with LDB and formalized as an interim structure called the SAF Centre of Leadership Development or SAF CLD, headed by a military officer who has held up to a Brigade-level Command appointment. The interim CLD retained the original LDB mission, which was to promote leadership excellence and to spearhead leadership development in the SAF. This mission was elaborated with the following roles that CLD would have to play in the SAF:

- Be the authority on leadership doctrine and training in the SAF;
- Co-ordinate, facilitate & monitor the effectiveness of leadership development efforts and systems across Services, Schools & Units;
- Collaborate with SAF HR agencies to synergize leadership education & training with career management & personnel development; and,
- Network with local and international agencies and institutions on new leadership theories and methods for leadership development.

At its inception, SAF CLD consisted of two Branches: a Leadership Training and Curriculum Branch staffed with military officers from the various Services and tasked to work closely with three Services to develop and align leadership development efforts, and, a Leadership Doctrine and Research Branch staffed by a mix of military and civilian behavioral scientists and tasked to develop the concepts and methodologies in the SAF's leadership development domain. Figure 2 illustrates the structure of SAF CLD when it was first established in December 2002. The "interim" status was adopted for SAF CLD pending a larger review and re-organization of the SAFTI Military Institute that was to occur from 2003 through to 2006/7.

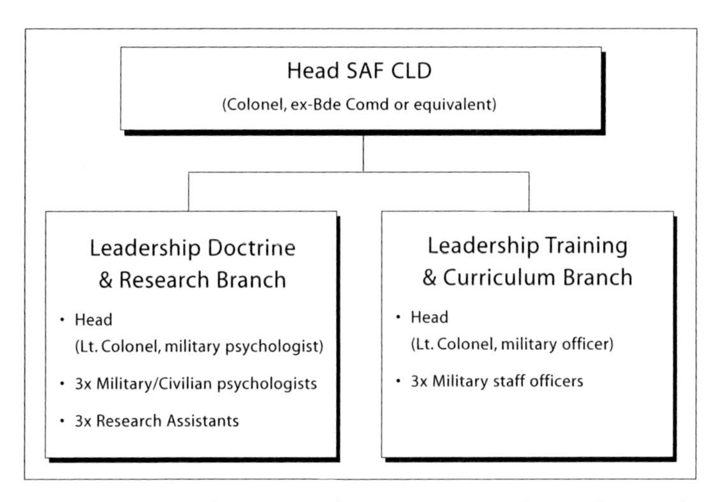

FIGURE 2: Original structure of Interim SAF CLD (December 2002).

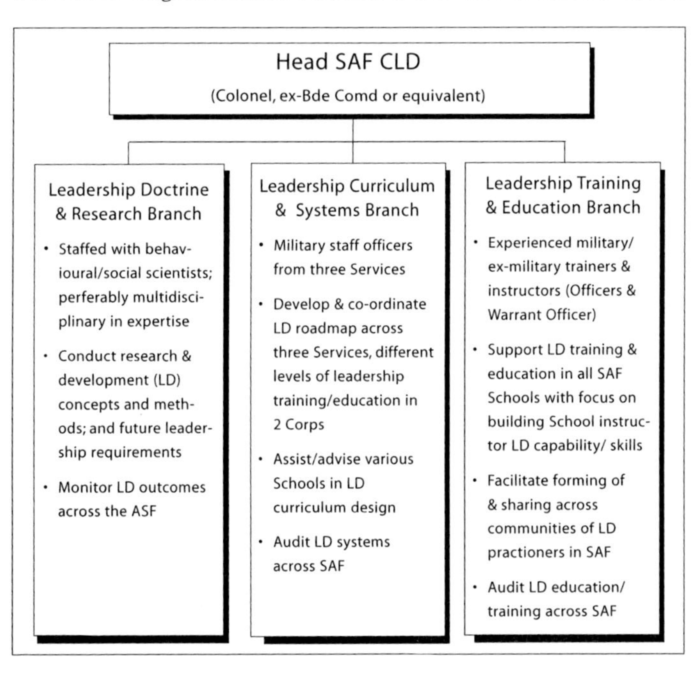

FIGURE 3. Expected, transformed structure of SAF CLD (from 2006 onwards).

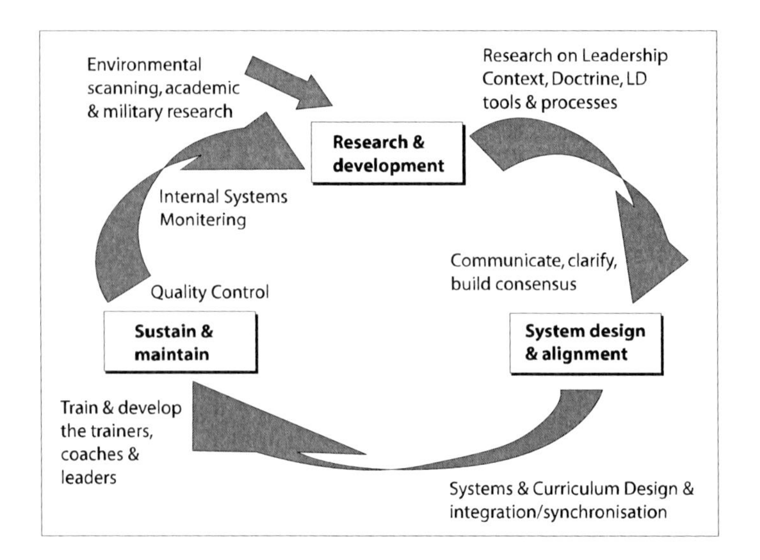

FIGURE 4: **Three reinforcing functions of the SAF Centre of Leadership Development.**

Today, as part of the overall transformation of SAFTI Military Institute, SAF CLD is expanding to include a separate Leadership Training and Education Branch while the original Leadership Training and Curriculum Branch is re-organizing into a "Leadership Curriculum and Systems Branch". The three Branches are organized to reflect the three reinforcing systems functions in the model depicted in Figure 4.

In 2003, its first year of operation, SAF CLD worked closely with the three Services to develop a Leadership Competency Model (LCM; see Table 1) to operationalize the "competency" component of the SAF Leadership Framework. The LCM improved on the original KAQ model by articulating the new "abilities" or behavioral competencies and skills at direct, organizational and strategic levels of leadership. It also introduced three new behavioral competency domains (conceptual, developmental, self/personal) that went beyond the people/social and task/mission-related domains emphasized in the original KAQ model. The idea was that implementation of the model would result in greater emphasis in the SAF on skills such as decision-making, ethical reasoning, coaching, team building, organization development, feedback, reflection, personal mastery and self-management, that are vital in the 3G SAF.

Competencies	"Core Behavioral Competencies" (for leader performance)				"Meta-Competency" (for growth)
	Conceptual Thinking	Social Competency	Mission Competency	Developmental Competency	Self meta-competency
Skills	Critical Thinking	Communicating to influence	Planning	Developing People	Personal Mastery
	Creative Thinking	Interpersonal Effectiveness	Decision making	Developing Team	Self-awarness
	Ethical Reasoning		Execution	Improving Organization	Self-management

TABLE 1: SAF Leadership Competencies and Skills

Besides competencies, CLD also introduced the academic and empirically-based "Full Range of Leadership" model to the SAF as a language to help SAF leaders think about and discuss "leadership styles" in the SAF. In the domain of "values", CLD also began to explore various new approaches to values inculcation and ethics education as a basis for new thinking on how to enhance SAF training effectiveness in these domains. In 2004, SAF CLD also began efforts to operationalize the "self" domain by articulating some principles for dealing with this delicate component of leadership.

Today, CLD's intention is to develop the domain of styles further by studying the different leadership styles that matter at different levels of leadership. For example, we believe that it may be more important to train our junior leaders in more transactional styles that can yield positive outcomes at their direct, face-to-face level of leadership. At higher levels, more change-oriented leadership styles are required.

In the past 4 years, CLD personnel have also learned many lessons in the experiments to implement Learning Organization practices and tools in the SAF.[8] It is now clearer to us that the overall strategy to enhance leadership development in the SAF must depend on both system design and the motivation and spirit of leaders themselves to engage in leadership development in the SAF. In 2005, CLD published a Monograph entitled *Spirit and Systems*[9] that called for a re-consideration of the SAF's spirit of leadership development within the larger context of the organization's transition from a modern, bureaucratic military to a post-modern, learning military force. For CLD, nurturing the Spirit of SAF Leaders is one of the purposes of the effort to transform the SAF into a Learning Organization. CLD is convinced that the idea of the SAF as a Learning Organization must go beyond merely creating conditions for organizational learning to produce a corps of SAF leaders that has the Spirit needed to drive leadership development in the SAF.

Focusing on *Development*: The Components of Systematic Leadership Development

In a recent review of industry best practices sponsored by the U.S. Army Research Institute for the Behavioral and Social Sciences, David Day and Stanley Halpin noted that successful leadership development depends more on consistent implementation of "best practices" rather than on the use of innovative practices.[10] They found that effective leadership development resulted from the systematic design of leadership development practices and tools into a learning process. They advocated that leadership development initiatives should be

[8] See S. Singh. "The Challenge of Building and Leading a Learning Army for the New Millennium" in *Pointer Supplement* (SAFTI Military Institute, March 2001).

[9] Chan, et al., Spirit and System.

[10] David V. Day, and Stanley M. Halpin, *Leadership Development: A Review of Industry Best Practices* (Technical Report 1111; Fort Leavenworth, KS: U.S. Army Research Institute Fort Leavenworth Research Unit, 2001), 55.

implemented as a systemic process and be used consistently throughout the training process because development occurs over time. Simply providing stand-alone leadership lessons or making people go through a developmental experience or administering a developmental feedback tool is not effective as the learning is not reinforced or integrated into the overall training program.

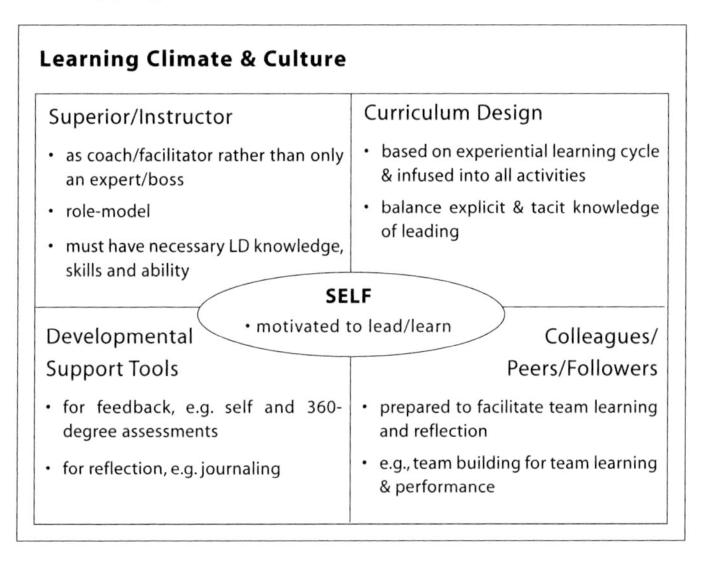

FIGURE 5: Design Components of a Leadership Development System

In 2001, CLD started to systematize leadership development in the SAF's Leadership Schools by integrating the best leadership development practices and tools into the overall training curriculum (e.g., when and how each leadership development initiative should be introduced and further reinforced throughout a training curriculum). CLD worked with the schools to conduct trials of the enhanced leadership development in various courses. These trials aimed to explore the effectiveness of systematic design of leadership development practices and tools which included learning organization principles and practices, team building, team learning, reflection and journaling in enhancing the leadership development experiences of trainees. The leadership development trials provided CLD with a better understanding of the design components and principles needed to guidesystematic leadership development in the SAF. Based on this, CLD developed a leadership development framework (see Figure 3) that comprises the following six design components to guide the design of systematic leadership development in an organization:[11]

- Component 1: The Self. The Self is at the core of the leadership development. This component refers to the trainee's personal involvement in the developmental process. Key to any development effort is the individual trainee's ownership and responsibility for his or her learning. An important assumption in leadership development is that the trainee is motivated to lead and motivated to learn in the first place. Unless the individual is self-motivated to learn, any effort to develop the individual will have limited returns. According to Popper, leadership is a function of one's ability and motivation to lead[12]. Although selection procedures (e.g., "expressed interest") may be used to identify leadership trainees who are motivated to lead and to learn, these should be complemented by training processes that strengthen the trainees' personal commitment to improve themselves and to grow as a leader (e.g., educating trainees on the developmental process, setting the right expectations, etc).

- Component 2: Superiors and Instructors who are Coaches and Facilitators. Superiors and instructors have direct influence over their trainees and subordinates, and therefore have natural impact on their leadership development. To date, the SAF has emphasized

[11] Kim-Yin Chan, et al., *Spirit and System*, 74.

[12] Micha Popper, "Main Principles and Practices in Leadership Development" in *Readings on How to Develop Leaders*, (SAFTI Military Institute Publication, October 2002), 4.

role modeling or leadership by example as a primary mechanism for superiors and instructors to influence their subordinates/trainees[13]. According to Popper, role modeling or learning by observation is a relatively passive method of leadership development. While this method is effective for behaviors that are specific and focused and can be practiced and replicated precisely, it may not be as effective for the inculcation of values, commitment and purpose. Superiors and leadership instructors need to take a more active role to inculcate values, commitment and purpose by engaging their trainees and subordinates in "joint investigations" which involve the "analysis of feelings, processing of information, and examining the considerations that led to certain decisions or behaviorial strategies".[14] Superiors and instructors should therefore see themselves equally as leader developers and not just subject matter experts in their specific fields. While they are technically and tactically competent in their vocation, they must also have the relevant leadership knowledge, skills and abilities to positively influence their subordinates/trainees. They should also play the role of coaches and facilitators if they are to actively assist in the leadership development of their subordinates and trainees. For this to happen, all superiors and instructors must be equipped with the necessary skills and tools to coach and facilitate development.

- Component 3: Peers, Colleagues & Subordinates. Leadership development can be more effective when there is team learning and feedback. In this aspect, peers and subordinates play an important role in developmental process through team learning[15]. Peers and

[13] Chan, et al., *Spirit and System*, 10

[14] Micha Popper, *Main Principles and Practices in Leadership Development*, 9.

[15] Robert N. Lussier and Christopher F. Achua, *Leadership: Theory, Application, Skill Building* (Cincinnati, Ohio: South-Western College Publishing, 2001), 257.

subordinates can act as a "Hall of Mirrors" to facilitate leadership development among trainees and leaders on the job[16]. As team members inspire, challenge, and build on each other's ideas through open sharing and feedback, their individual learning is enhanced. For team learning and open feedback to happen, it is necessary to facilitate team building for team learning in all learning groups or syndicates in schools. Team building should also be introduced in units not only for team performance but also to encourage team learning of leadership and team processes.

- Component 4: Curriculum Design. The process of leadership development is based on the experiential learning cycle in which every leadership development effort is systematically designed into a continuous learning process of conceptual understanding, practice, observation, feedback and reflection[17]. In designing the training curricula, it will be beneficial to connect abstract concepts with active experimentation, concrete experience, and reflective observation[18]. For example, learning can begin with a conceptual understanding of a particular aspect of leadership. It remains, however, as knowledge. Unless time and opportunities are created for practicing, observing and reflecting, the understanding would not deepen further and learning would be superficial and limited. When effort is given to observing and practicing the associated skills, the experience forms the basis for subsequent reflection, which further aids in developing a better conceptual understanding of leadership. Feedback from peers and instructors on the practice can make the reflection more effective as blind

[16] Micha Popper, *Main Principles and Practices in Leadership Development*, 10.

[17] David Kolb, *Experiential learning: Experience is the source of learning and development* (Englewood Cliffs, NJ: Prentice Hall, 1983).

[18] Richard L. Hughes, Robert C. Ginnett and Gordon J. Curphy. *Leadership: Enhancing the lessons of experience*, 5th ed. (Boston: Irwin McGraw-Hill, 2006).

areas, which the trainees may have failed to observe or notice, are highlighted. Finally, leadership training should incorporate a balance of the explicit and the tacit knowledge of leadership in our military context. Providing training on real life leadership issues and future-oriented leadership competencies will not only make the training more credible to the leadership trainees but also help them prepare for actual and future leadership challenges in the units[19].

- Component 5: Developmental Tools & Procedures. While the social components (e.g., instructors/superiors, colleagues/peers) of the leadership development system are key driving mechanisms, it is important to support the developmental process with basic tools such as self-assessments, peer appraisal and 360-degree feedback, personal and team journal[20]. The "tools" can also include procedures that facilitate leadership or command effectiveness and development, for example, processes that facilitate the preparation for command and command transition, and the facilitation of learning through after action reviews, etc.

- Component 6: Learning Climate & Culture. This refers to the immediate learning environment and the extent to which it is conducive for personal learning, growth and change. The assumption is that integrating organizational learning practices and tools (e.g., personal and social practices and disciplines such as having rules for quality conversations, deep listening and reflection that facilitate individual, team and organizational-level learning) with the leadership development for example

---

[19] David V. Day and Stanley M. Halpin, Leadership Development: A Review of Industry Best Practices, 11.

[20] Cynthia D. McCauley, Russ S. Moxley and Ellen Van Velsor, eds., *The Centre for Creative Leadership Handbook of Leadership Development* (San Francisco: Jossey-Bass, 1998).

would create a learning climate and culture conducive for enriching trainees' leadership development experiences.

This leadership development framework serves as a useful guide for the systematic design of an enriching developmental process in terms of a generic set of leadership development practices and tools that may be used in any leadership courses or work processes. The challenge, however, remains in the need for instructors and commanders to shift their thinking of leadership development from that of an isolated set of lessons or activities in a training curriculum, to a more process-oriented experiential approach. To date, the SAF has made a significant effort to better integrate the "softer", behavioral "leadership curriculum" with the vocational curriculum (e.g., operational military knowledge, military technology and strategic studies) in its leadership schools. The Schools are enlarging its current training-oriented philosophy to include development (i.e., inspiring, training and educating leaders) and building relationships. Military training curricula are also being redesigned to ensure that leadership training is oriented toward preparing and inspiring SAF leaders for the future SAF context and not just the present. More importantly, the Schools are beginning to invest the time, resources and systemic structures in instructors' education and training to support leadership development. School instructors are being trained to use the SAF doctrinal definition and framework for leadership as well as the principles for leadership development as starting points to re-frame their leadership development assumptions and practices acquired tacitly from personal experience and role modeling over the years.

Discussion: SAF CLD's "Value-added"

Looking back at the past 4 years of SAF CLD's existence, we believe that these are some of our most significant "value-added" to the SAF:

- More strategic alignment of leadership development in the SAF. We believe that SAF CLD has provided greater tri-service, senior leadership, cross-School, School-to-unit, HR-and-training-system alignment, coordination and integration in leadership development through a common Framework, concepts, models, leadership directives, guides, pamphlets, a centralized SAF Leadership Development Committee, and a CLD intranet website. Most significantly, SAF CLD's development of the SAF Leadership Competency Model (LCM) is now being considered by the SAF's human resource agencies as a basis for a fundamental re-design of the SAF human resource system.

- Greater integration, customization and rationalization of both leadership doctrine and Leadership Development methods. This includes the adaptation of methods such as competency-based learning, Organizational Learning (OL), team-building, and coaching to the SAF's unique needs in peacetime and operations, for the present and the future, and for a wider-spectrum of Operations.

- Initiatives that serve to fill "gaps" in SAF's Leadership Development system. For example, CLD's initiatives to work with SAFTI-MI Schools to look into the quality of the SAF's education on matters related to "officership" and "military ethics." CLD has also brought to the SAF's awareness new and relevant military leadership development concerns by organizing workshops and seminars for key SAF Senior Leaders and the training community on topics such as "battle command," the "human in command," "leadership styles," and "resilience."

- Greater leverage for SAF. This was evident in SAF CLD's efforts to source for higher quality and more customized leadership development programs and research the SAF from external training providers, experts and Universities.

- Greater local and international networking for SAFTI-MI and the SAF in the domain of Leadership Development. SAF CLD has actively participated at various international forums. For example, at the International Applied Military Psychology Symposium (IAMPS) where it was awarded a "Best paper" by Division 19 of the American Psychological Association in 2004, and at the annual International Military Testing Association (IMTA) conference, where in 2005, we presented five empirical papers and research proposals in collaboration with the Nanyang Business School. In November 2005, SAF CLD also hosted a 1-day meeting of international military leadership centres in Singapore, which was an idea initiated at a visit to the Canadian Forces Leadership Institute (CFLI). The plan is to organize a follow-up meeting of leadership centres in Canada in October 2006, when CFLI hosts the next IMTA conference.

Conclusion

Overall, we believe that SAF CLD's main contribution has been to create the conditions for more systematic leadership development in the SAF as envisaged in the 2002 SAF Leadership Development Masterplan. When compared to the past approach where MINDEF psychologists supported the SAF in leadership development outside of LDB, we believe that CLD has more effectively acted as the SAF's internal common resource to drive more strategic and systematic military leadership development throughout the organization. It has achieved this because of a closer linkage to the SAF training system and a more-focused understanding of the SAF's unique leadership development challenges and needs. Looking ahead, SAF CLD will work towards greater international collaboration in the area of military leadership development, perhaps in the sharing of leadership development knowledge, methods & tools, and possibly in joint research on the cross-cultural context of coalition and multinational military operations.

To conclude, with changes in the security environment, more than ever the SAF is today a "24-7" military force – one that has to maintain a high state of readiness for a wide spectrum of operations 24 hours a day, 7 days a week. With improvements in technology and education in our society, the SAF is also transforming itself to be a "3G" military force – one with enhanced capabilities via the exploitation of new concepts and technologies, and, an improved ability to fight across a wider spectrum of operations. It is in this context that the SAF has invested in the a new Centre of Leadership Development to spearhead the development of competent, adaptive and self-aware leaders who influence soldiers based on an understanding of the SAF's mission, appreciate the complex operating environment, and, who act to achieve desired outcomes on the basis of the SAF Core Values – what we now call SAF Leadership 24-7.

CONTRIBUTORS

Dr. **Jamie Cullens** has been the Director of the Centre for Defence Leadership Studies since 2002. He is a former Infantry officer and has also worked in the resources industry.

Air Commodore **Peter W. Gray** is the Director of the Defence Leadership and Management Centre at the Defence Academy of the United Kingdom.

Jonathan Harvey is the Senior Research Analyst within the Defence Leadership and Management Centre at the Defence Academy of the United Kingdom.

Colonel, Dr. **Bernd Horn** is the Director of the Canadian Forces Leadership Institute (CFLI). He is an experienced infantry officer with command experience at the unit and sub-unit level. He was the Commanding Officer of 1 RCR (2001-2003); the Officer Commanding 3 Commando, the Canadian Airborne Regiment (1993-1995); and the Officer Commanding "B" Company, 1 RCR (1992-1993). He is also an Adjunct-Associate Professor of History at the Royal Military College of Canada.

Commander **Peter Kelly** is the Deputy Director of the Centre and is a serving Navy officer with a background in education.

Lieutenant-Colonel, Dr. **Allister MacIntyre** has been with the CFLI since 2001. He completed his PhD and Master's degrees in Psychology at Queen's University. From 1993 until 1996 he served as the Chair of the *Psychology in the Military* section of the Canadian Psychological Association. He is presently an adjunct professor at Carleton University, and the University of Guelph and will be leaving the military in 2006 to take up a position as an Associate Professor at the Royal Military College in Kingston, Ontario.

Colonel **Sukhmohinder Singh** is a Commando Officer by vocation. He is currently the Head of the SAF Centre of Leadership Development (CLD), and concurrently the Head of Army Curriculum Branch at SAFTI Military Institute. He was instrumental in developing the SAF's strategy for enhancing leadership training and development among its officers, in its transformation towards a "3G SAF" concept. COL Sukh holds a BA (History & Political Science) from the National University of Singapore. He also has a Graduate Diploma in Organizational Learning. He has attended U.S. Ranger, Pathfinder, and Special Forces training. He has commanded an Infantry Battalion, 3 SIR, and the 10th Singapore Infantry Brigade. He served as the Head of SAF Advanced Schools and Commander of Army Advanced Officer School prior to assuming his appointment as Head of the SAF Centre of Leadership Development in January 2003. He has previously published in the *Pointer: Journal of the Singapore Armed Forces*.

Lieutenant-Colonel, Dr. **Kim-Yin Chan** is currently the Head of Leadership Doctrine and Research Branch, at the SAF Centre of Leadership Development. He is an Infantry Officer by training, and has commanded at the platoon and company levels. He received his BSc in Psychology with First Class Honors from the University of London, U.K., in 1988, and his MA and Ph.D. in Industrial-Organizational Psychology from the University of Illinois at Urbana-Champaign, USA, in 1997 and 1999. He has published academic research papers in the *Journal of Applied Psychology, Journal of Vocational Behavior, Personnel Psychology, Multivariate Behavioral Research*, the *Journal of Education and Measurement Research, Pointer: Journal of the SAF*, and *Catalyst: Journal of the Military Behavioral Sciences in MINDEF and the SAF.* He has also presented at several international conferences, and is currently an Adjunct Associate Professor at the Nanyang Business School, Nanyang Technological University.

Kwee-Hoon Lim, is a Field Psychologist at the SAF Centre of Leadership Development, at the SAFTI Military Institute. She was previously commissioned as a Personnel Officer, and held several appointments in an Infantry Brigade and the SAF Signal formation, MINDEF Education Department, and the Applied Behavioral Sciences Department in MINDEF. She received her BA in Psychology, graduating with Honors from the University of Calgary, Canada, in 1989. She has a Graduate Diploma in Training and Development from the University of Sheffield, UK. She published in an in-house journal called *Synergy*, and also co-authored a book entitled *Problem Solving Toolkits: Simplified for Beginners*, published in 1999.

GLOSSARY

1G SAF	First Generation SAF
2G SAF	Second Generation SAF
3G SAF	Third Generation SAF
ACE	Allied Command Europe
ACSC	Australian Command and Staff Course
ADC	Australian Defence College
ADF	Australian Defence Force
ADFA	Australian Defence Force Academy
ADM (HR Mil)	Assistant Deputy Minister Human Resources Military
AIF	First Australian Imperial Force
AMF(L)	ACE Mobile Force (Land)
ANZAC	Australian and New Zealand Army Corps
BRNC	Britannia Royal Naval College at Dartmouth
CDA	Canadian Defence Academy
CDCLMS	Centre for Defence Command Leadership and Management Studies
CDS	Chief of the Defence Staff
CDLS	Centre for Defence Leadership Studies
CF	Canadian Forces
CFLI	Canadian Forces Leadership Institute
CLD	Centre of Leadership Development
CPO	Chief Petty Officer
DC	Defence Committee
DLC	Defence Leadership Centre
DLMC	Defence Leadership and Management Centre
DLN	Defence Leadership Network
DND	Department of National Defence
DSLP	Defence Strategic Leadership Programme
DTR	Defence Training Review
EI	Emotional Intelligence

HQ	Headquarters
INTERFET	International Force East Timor
IAMPS	International Applied Military Psychology Symposium
IMTA	International Military Testing Association
JLD	Joint Leadership Doctrine
JMAP	Joint Method of Military Appreciation
KAQ	Knowledge, Abilities and Qualities
LCM	Leadership Competency Model
LDB	Leadership Development Branch
MINDEF	Ministry of Defence
MMC	Minister's Monitoring Committee on Change in the Department of National Defence and the Canadian Forces
MND	Minister of National Defence
MOD	Ministry of Defence
NATO	North Atlantic Treaty Organization
NCO	Non-Commissioned Officer
NCW	Network Centric Warfare
OIC	Officer in Charge
OL	Organizational Learning
PAR	Personnel Assessment
PD	Professional Development
PLICIT	Professionalism, Loyalty, Integrity, Courage, Innovation and Teamwork
RAAF	Royal Australian Air Force
RAF	Royal Air Force
RAN	Royal Australian Navy

RMAS	Royal Military Academy at Sandhurst
SAF	Singapore Armed Forces
SAF Leadership 24-7	SAF Leadership Framework
SAFTI	Singapore Armed Forces Training Institute
SAFTI-MI	SAFTI Military Institute
SLG	Senior Leadership Group
UK	United Kingdom
UN	United Nations
UNTAET	United Nations Transitional Administration in East Timor
US	United States
VBL	Values-Based Leadership

INDEX